Harriet E. Michael

PRAYER

It's Not About You

Harriet E. Michael
Psalm 113:3

Prayer: It's Not About You

© 2016 Harriet E. Michael

ISBN-13: 978-1-944120-00-9
ISBN-10: 1-944120-00-9
E-book ISBN-13: 978-1-944120-01-6

Unless otherwise noted, Scriptures are taken from the Holy Bible, New International Version®, NIV®. Copyright © 1973, 1978, 1984, 2011 by Biblica, Inc.™ Used by permission of Zondervan. All rights reserved worldwide. www.zondervan.com.

Scriptures marked "ESV" are from *The Holy Bible,* English Standard Version® (ESV®), copyright © 2001 by Crossway, a publishing ministry of Good News Publishers. Used by permission. All rights reserved.

Scriptures marked "KJV" are from *The Holy Bible*, the Authorized (King James) Version.

Scriptures marked" NASB" are from *The Holy Bible,* New American Standard Bible. Copyright © 1960, 1962, 1963, 1968, 1971, 1972, 1973, 1975, 1977, 1995 by The Lockman Foundation.

Scripture quotations marked "NKJV" are taken from The New King James Version / Thomas Nelson Publishers, Nashville: Thomas Nelson Publishers., Copyright © 1982. Used by permission. All rights reserved.

Scripture quotations marked "HCSB" are taken from the Holman Christian Standard Bible (HCSB) Copyright © 1999, 2000, 2002, 2003, 2009 by Holman Bible Publishers, Nashville, Tennessee. All rights reserved.

Scripture quotations marked "NRSV" are taken from New Revised Standard Version Bible, copyright © 1989 the Division of Christian Education of the National Council of the Churches of Christ in the United States of America. Used by permission. All rights reserved.

Published by Pix-N-Pens Publishing, 2631 Holly Springs Pkwy, Box 35, Holly Springs, GA 30142.

www.PixNPens.com

Dedication

I dedicate this book to my four wonderful children,
who have given me much experience in the practice of prayer.
You are such blessings to me!

Table of Contents

Chapter 1: Why Pray?

Some years ago, my local newspaper printed an article about prayer. It contained interviews with several ministers including clergy and leaders from a number of different religious groups: a Protestant pastor, a Catholic Priest, a Jewish Rabbi, and a Muslim Imam. This may sound like a set up for a joke but it wasn't. It was a serious article about the role of prayer in today's world. These religious leaders held an open discussion about their beliefs regarding the practice and effectiveness of prayer. They all agreed that prayer was a wonderful personal exercise and discipline but, unfortunately, it had no real power. Though it was not believed to impact circumstances, prayer was still viewed by this group as an activity that offered emotional benefits for the one praying, such as comfort and consolation. Their conclusion, drawn from many years of ministry, was that though soothing, prayer was powerless. These religious leaders nonetheless strongly endorsed prayer for its mental health benefits.

A picture of hands folded next to a flickering candle accompanied the article. It appeared so sweet, so cozy, so soothing, but according to the article, so utterly useless. If their conclusion is correct, praying people would benefit as much from any other self-comforting technique. One may as well soak in a warm tub or drink hot tea as to pray.

I cannot make my fears disappear that easily. A cup of hot tea doesn't do it for me—so I pray. And praying does not always make me feel better. At times prayer is agonizing because it increases my awareness of the pain or ugliness of a situation.

Why do I pray then? I pray because I am convinced prayer really does have the power to impact the situation that concerns me. Prayer plays an important role in God's plan for bringing about His purposes on earth. Does God need my prayers? No, of course not! God does not need anything, but because He loves me, He allows you and me to participate in His work.

My personal quest for understanding

As a child, I learned to pray as part of a daily routine. These were the simple "God bless" types of prayers. But as life took its inevitable twists and turns, some of which have been extremely difficult, I found myself longing for a better understanding of prayer. I believed in the power of prayer but I wanted to know how to *really* do it. I looked deeper into the Scripture seeking to know what the Bible said about prayer. I wished to pray more effectively. I have learned much and now have some understanding as to why prayer might be a powerless tool in the hands of some people, like the ministers in my newspaper article believed. On the other hand, I have also learned that prayer is a mighty weapon in the hands of a believer who understands and uses it correctly.

The Bible passage that first prompted me to think about prayer is found in 1 Kings 16-18. In this passage, Elijah prays for rain after the miracle on Mount Carmel. Let me set the stage by reviewing the story.

Ahab, a wicked man, had become king over Israel. He did more evil in the sight of the Lord than all who had come before him. Because of this, God caused a terrible drought in the land. Then, in 1 Kings 18:19-44, Elijah tells Ahab to gather all of Israel along with the prophets of Baal and of Asherah, and to meet him on Mount Carmel. Perhaps you remember the miracle God did there. All 850 false prophets failed in their attempt to call fire from heaven to burn the sacrifice they had made. For an entire day, they were unable to get their god's attention despite shouting, gesturing, and even cutting themselves. Then, it was Elijah's turn. He soaked his sacrifice with water before he even began to ask God to send fire. Since it was a time of severe drought, water was scarce and precious. Isn't it interesting that Elijah poured out what was precious, before God showed His great miraculous power? Finally, Elijah prayed for God to send down fire from heaven, and God did—instantly! God's fire consumed everything, even the stones, dust, and water.

As amazing as this prayer and its resulting miracle are, it is Elijah's next prayer, the prayer for rain, which fascinates me more. After the miracle of fire but before he prayed for the rain, Elijah told King Ahab, "Go, eat and drink, for there is the sound of a heavy rain." Apparently, Elijah believed the rain would come before he even prayed for it. But he prayed nonetheless. He crouched down, put his face between his knees, and prayed. We know he was praying, and not just bending down, from James 5:18.

After a time, he sent his servant Gehazi to look for signs of rain and report back to him. Elijah remained in an attitude of prayer. The servant soon returned with the news that there was no sign of rain. Elijah sent Gehazi out again and again. Finally, on the seventh time, Gehazi returned with the news that he had spotted a tiny cloud in the sky, not a major storm coming, or even several clouds—just one small cloud. But this was enough for Elijah. He told his servant to tell King Ahab that he had better hurry on his journey before the rain started.

First Kings 18:45 says the sky grew black with clouds, the wind rose, and heavy rain started falling.

This story gave me pause. I found myself contemplating many points. Why did Elijah have to pray for the rain? He already knew God was going to send it. He had even told King Ahab that rain was coming. Why didn't he just take the coming rain for granted? Why did he crouch down low asking God for what he already knew God was going to do? Why did he do it seven times? Why did it not start raining the minute Elijah began praying? According to James 5:17, Elijah prayed earnestly. Why? Why the earnestness? Why not just matter of fact prayer? Elijah knew what was going to happen. He knew God was about to send the long awaited, hoped for rain. Yet, somehow, earnest prayer was necessary.

I do not offer definitive answers to these questions, but I have drawn some conclusions:

1) God commands us to pray. Prayer is a matter of obedience. God is glorified when we see His power through answered prayer.

2) Prayer is important. It is as if prayer is a catalyst by which God's plan is brought about.

3) Prayer does not change God's plan, rather it helps to bring that plan into action. Is the success of God's plan dependent upon our prayer? Of course not! If we do not pray, is God somehow helpless to enact that plan? No. We are not that powerful, and God is never powerless to do as He pleases. God cannot be limited. Job 42:2 tells us that no plan of God's can be thwarted. Yet, because of His love for us, God allows us the privilege of participating in His plan. Prayer is work to be done and He invites us to do it.

4) Prayer has value. Prayer can bring about changes in people and situations. It does not change God's plan, but it does bring about changes in the world to accord with that plan. Yes, prayer is actually effective. It is not, as the ministers in my newspaper article thought, only a comforting technique.

5) We need to be tenacious in our prayers. Elijah kept praying and sending his servant to look for God's answer. Like Elijah, we should eagerly watch for answers to our prayers too. Psalm 5:3 says "…in the morning I lay my requests before you and wait expectantly."

6) God answers prayers. He sent rain when Elijah prayed—not before. This promised rain was sent in response to Elijah's earnest prayers.

7) We should be prepared for how prayer will affect our lives. Elijah ran to the city of Jezreel as the heavy rains fell. No doubt when he arrived, he was soaked to the bone!

My understanding of prayer has also been shaped through personal experiences. It seems the job God has given me repeatedly throughout my life has been that of ministering to, agonizing over, and praying for loved ones who were in trouble. Often these troubles were brought on by sin. Much of my life I have found myself standing next to fires, so to speak, trying to put them out. Some of the situations have been dire. I found myself praying desperately, longing to understand prayer better and to pray more effectively.

Charles Stanley, in his book *When the Enemy Strikes,* gives a brief description of the fiery darts or flaming arrows common to Roman battles. Paul referred to these in Ephesians 6:16 when he told us to "take up the shield of faith with which you can extinguish all the flaming arrows of the evil one." Stanley writes, "In such a rain of flaming arrows, it was very difficult for a soldier to keep from being hit. And even if he did avoid a direct hit, he had to deal with fire all around him."[1] This is a good description of my life. Many times, I have found myself with "fire all around me." This fire was spiritual fire, which often threatened to consume people and things that were dear to me.

Through these experiences, God has taught me about prayer. This book is an attempt to record what I have learned for the benefit of others. This book will look at prayer and prayer warriors from the Bible to see how the various Biblical characters prayed. It will cover what they said, how they approached God, under what circumstances they prayed, and what their lives were like. The book will also discuss some general teachings about prayer in the Scriptures. We will learn specific principles and practices from the Bible that can be applied to our lives so that we can become more effective prayer warriors.

QUESTIONS FOR REFLECTION

Does prayer have any real power?

Does prayer change God's plan or does it change the people and circumstances around us to accord with God's plan?

Do our prayers provoke God to act on our behalf in accordance with His great plan? (Did God act before, after, or *as* Elijah prayed?)

How do the other prayer warriors in the Bible pray? Are there any common threads running through all of these prayers?

OLD TESTAMENT

"We have taken a wartime walkie-talkie and tried to turn it into a civilian intercom to call the servants for another cushion in the den." [1]
John Piper in *Desiring God*

Chapter 2: Moses

The first prayer warrior in the Old Testament, and perhaps my favorite, is Moses. For the purposes of this book, we will look at how he conducted himself in his role as intercessor for the children of Israel. Nonetheless, a brief recapping of his life is helpful in order to understand how he came into this role of intercessor.

While the Jewish people were enslaved by the Egyptians around 1500 BC,[1] the baby Moses' mother, fearing for his life, hid him in a basket. Pharaoh's daughter found the baby, floating in the Nile River. She took him home with her, adopting him, and bringing him up in the palace. This story of the baby Moses is found in Exodus 2:1-9. Acts 7:21-24 adds that growing up, Moses was instructed in all the wisdom of the Egyptians and mighty in his words and deeds.

Reading through to chapter four of Exodus, we find more of Moses' story. When he was forty years old, he decided to visit his brothers, the children of Israel. Seeing one of them wronged, he attempted to defend the oppressed man and ended up killing the aggressor. Frightened, Moses fled to the wilderness where he married a woman named Zipporah and later had a son. Finding a wife, marrying, and having a child must have taken several years. Perhaps he would have lived out his life in obscurity if God had not spoken to him in a burning bush, changing his life forever. God told Moses He had seen the affliction of His people in Egypt and would deliver them. He instructed Moses to go to Pharaoh and bring His people out of their captivity in Egypt.

Moses responded in a manner that was anything but exemplary. The conversation, paraphrased, went something like this:

Moses: "Who am I, that I should go to Pharaoh?"

God: "I'll be with you."

Moses: "The people will want to know who you are. What is your name?"

God: "I AM who I AM."

Then God told Moses what to expect, but assured him that God would be with him. Moses complained that the people still would not believe him, so God gave him signs and wonders to perform. Still Moses objected, arguing that he was not an eloquent speaker.

But God reminded Moses that He had made Moses' mouth, He would give him the words to say.

Even after all of this, in Exodus 4:13, Moses said, "Please send someone else."

When Moses said this, he spoke so candidly with God. This honesty in his conversations with God is something we see repeatedly. He told God all of his fears and doubts, and sometimes he even argued. We should be just as honest in our conversations with God.

Isn't it interesting to see how God works? When Moses was the adopted grandson of Pharaoh, schooled in the wisdom of the day and powerful in both his speech and actions, according to Acts 7:22, God did not find him useful. But when he was a broken man, fearful and only hoping to live a quiet life with no one knowing who he was, that's when God found him useful. When Moses thought he could save his people himself, like he did in Acts 7:25, God thought differently. But when Moses realized he was not capable, God used him to rescue not just one Hebrew, but the entire nation. God's plans are always bigger than our plans and He often uses us best after we are broken. Perhaps because when we are broken, we are more submissive.

Why did God choose Moses? He was not eloquent, confident, or even eager. He seemed the least likely choice for such an important job. Numbers 12:3 helps us understand why God chose him. Moses was a humble man. The Bible says he was more humble than anyone else on the face of the earth. God loves to elevate the humble. He loves to give them jobs they think they cannot do. My oldest son jokingly says that if God has called a person to do a work for Him, it doesn't speak well for that person in human terms. My son is right. Moses was a frightened murderer with no self-confidence who just wanted to live out his life in obscurity, away from trouble.

David was not only a shepherd, according to 1 Samuel 16:6-11, he was the youngest and least likely of all of Jesse's sons to be anointed as the next king. David's mighty men were a group of outcasts. First Samuel 22:2 tells us that the men who gathered around David were, "those who were in distress or in debt or discontented." Samuel was a small child when he heard God's call according to the third chapter of 1 Samuel. Joshua 2:1 says that Rahab was a prostitute, Matthew 4:18 tells us that the disciples were fishermen, and on it goes.

The Bible is full of examples of God using the most unlikely people for His work. When someone becomes great in God's work, a mighty leader like Moses for instance, people can know it is not as a result of that person's own power or influence, but of God's. In Isaiah 42:8 God says, "I am the Lord; that is my name! I will not yield my glory to another."

As a child, I lived with missionary parents in Nigeria, West Africa.

I remember my father sharing his thoughts on sheep and goats. Both animals wandered around aimlessly. It was difficult to tell them apart. They were a nuisance. My dad said when he first came to Nigeria he was bothered by the fact that in the Scripture sheep are depicted favorably while goats are cast in an unfavorable light. For example, in Matthew 25:31-41, Jesus talked of separating the sheep from the goats at the end of time. He said He will put the sheep on His right hand, and the goats on His left. Then He will tell the sheep on His right to come to Him because they are blessed of His Father. But the goats on His left will be told to depart into the eternal fire prepared for the devil and his angels because they are cursed.

My father's consternation came from his experience with these animals. When sheep and goats were observed wandering about unattended, the goats appeared more intelligent. Sheep seemed quite dumb. If my father accidentally hit one while driving, it was always a sheep. They did not have even enough sense to get out of the way of a moving vehicle. Sheep often wandered into the road just as a car was coming. Goats, on the other hand, were aware of danger and avoided it.

Initially, my dad almost felt insulted that God called His people sheep. Then one day he realized why God wanted us to be like sheep. Sheep are trusting of their shepherd and completely lost without him. Goats are competent on their own but they are so self-reliant they cannot be led.[2] This, then, is the trait God looks for in those He calls to do His work, and prayer is part of that work. God wants us to be completely dependent on Him, not on ourselves. This certainly was true of Moses. Keenly aware of his own limitations, Moses had no personal confidence. Because of his doubt and fear, he even resisted the work God called him, yet he still obeyed God's orders.

Moses as an intercessor

One of the first times Moses interceded before God on behalf of others is recorded in Exodus 17:8-16, which tells of a battle that occurred during the trip to the Promised Land. In the story, Israel experienced an unprovoked attack. This classic picture of intercession gives us insight into spiritual battles. Moses told Joshua to choose some men to join him in the battle. With Joshua and his men fighting below, Moses stood atop a hill, away from the actual battle, and lifted up his hands and staff to God. When Moses' arms were up, Israel's side seemed to be winning, but if his arms lowered, the enemy prevailed. How long can a person hold his arms up? Moses' arms grew tired and he needed help. So, two men stood on either side of Moses to help keep his hands up. Finally, the battle ended with Israel victorious.

In this story, the struggle was on three levels. First, there was an actual battle involving hand-to-hand combat in which people were physically wounded and killed. On the second level was an intercessor (Moses) who lifted his hands towards God as he asked God for help in the battle. Moses grew weary as the battle lingered even though his perseverance was essential for victory. The third level of struggle involved the men who came alongside Moses to help him with his work.

I have experienced times when I have seen this interplay of activities in my own life. There was a point when someone I loved became the victim of another person's sin. It was completely unprovoked and totally unexpected. Like the Israelites, my loved one was merely traveling along on her journey of life, when an opposing, destructive force came against her. Left struggling in many areas of her life, she suffered physically, emotionally, and spiritually. She lost her sense of self-worth, her ability to trust others, and for a brief time, even her faith. She became severely depressed but as her depression improved, it was replaced with anger and rebellion. This battle lasted a long time and became progressively worse for several months before things began to improve. There were numerous months of counseling and other types of intervention.

When all was said and done, God used all that He had allowed into her life to strengthen her faith and to make her a deeper, stronger, and more compassionate person. During this difficult time, my loved one played the Joshua role as she fought the battle on a personal level. I played the Moses role. I lifted her up daily before the Lord. Like Moses, I sometimes grew weary. Thankfully, like Moses' friends who held his arms up, some close friends of mine came alongside of me to pray with me, comfort me, and encourage me to keep interceding for my loved one.

The next time we see Moses interceding for the Israelites is in Exodus 32-34. This is actually a protracted story and we will only touch on certain highlights. Chapter 32 finds Moses on Mount Sinai communing with God and receiving the Ten Commandments. With Moses still on the mountain, God saw the people in the valley below making and worshiping a golden calf. God told Moses to go down to the people because they had corrupted themselves. In verse nine, God calls the people stiff-necked. The New American Standard Bible uses the term obstinate. God says they angered Him and He wants to destroy them and instead make a great nation from Moses.

Here is another example of why God chose Moses for the job of intercessor—Moses loved the people more than himself. God already knew the nature of these people. He knew they were obstinate before

He brought them out of Egypt. He also knew Moses would not agree to His offer to create a new nation from Moses' line. God never really intended to do this. His suggestion to Moses served the dual purpose of testing Moses and at the same time prompting him to intercede on behalf of the people. God knew His promise to Abraham, Isaac, and Jacob. He did not need to be reminded, but apparently, He wanted to be reminded. God has worked prayer into the formula for bringing about His will. This is an example of God prompting someone to pray for another. He prompted Moses to intercede on behalf of the children of Israel. He wanted Moses to do exactly what Moses did—to ask Him not to pour out His anger on the people.

In Ezekiel 22:30-31, we see God looking for an intercessor. In that verse God says, "I looked for someone among them who would build up the wall and stand before me in the gap on behalf of the land so I would not destroy it, but I found no one. So I will pour out my wrath on them and consume them with my fiery anger."

Moses did exactly what God wanted him to do. Exodus 32:11-14 tells us Moses interceded, saying, "Why should your anger burn against your people whom you have brought out of Egypt with great power and a mighty hand?" He asked God to turn from his fierce anger and not bring disaster on the people. He reminded God of His promises, saying, "Remember your servants Abraham, Isaac and Israel to whom you swore by yourself: 'I will make your descendants as numerous as the stars in the sky and I will give your descendants all this land.'" Then, in verse 14, we read that God relented and did not bring disaster on the people.

As the story continues Moses goes down from the mountain, sees the golden calf and becomes angry. He breaks the stone tablets, and asks the Levites to enact punishment on the people. But he also tells the people in Exodus 32:30, "You have committed a great sin. But now I will go up to the Lord; perhaps I can make atonement for your sin." Again, Moses went before the Lord and asked for forgiveness for the people.

It is important to note that the people were not repentant. They had not asked Moses to intercede for them, but he did anyway because he was burdened by their sin. Then Moses did an interesting thing. He asked to be allowed to perish along with the people if they were not forgiven. This demonstrated what a great leader Moses really was. He truly cared more about the people than he did about himself. He would rather have died with his people than to live after God destroyed them, even when that destruction was coupled with an offer to make a new nation from his line. This kind of love for people is exactly why God chose Moses for this job. God loved the people too, so He prompted Moses to intercede for them.

In this interaction, Moses petitioned God to stay true to His plans. Like Jesus in Mathew 6:10, Moses essentially told God, "your will be done." Moses *knew* God's will because God had already made it known through the promises made to Abraham, Isaac, and Jacob. Based on these promises, Moses interceded bravely for the people, and God answered in a big way. God did not let their sin go unpunished but He did not abandon His promise, either. After dealing with their sin, God fulfilled His promise to the people in Exodus 33:2-3 by sending His angel before them to drive out the Canaanites, the Amorites, the Hittites, the Perizzites, Hivites, and the Jubusites. God answered Moses' request not only favorably but also abundantly.

However, God added one more thing. God told Moses that He

would not go with him because the people were still obstinate, and they might provoke Him to destroy them along the way. And again, in Exodus 33:12-15, Moses interceded, asking God to go with them. Moses had not taken the bait to have the people destroyed, or to have himself glorified. He laid himself on the line for these people, and he was not going to settle for God's blessings without God's presence.

People often want God's blessings more than they want God's presence. This was not true of Moses. He knew what we all should know, without God's presence and His abiding Spirit, everything else is worthless. So Moses reminded God again that these were His people and if His presence would not go with them, then Moses didn't want God to bring them out. Then he asked God how would other nations know that these people were God's people, if God was not with them?

Moses appealed to God based on the glory of God's own name. This is an appropriate way to appeal to God and we will see it repeated in Scripture. In Exodus 34:9, Moses prayed, "If I have found favor in your eyes, then let the Lord go with us. Although this is a stiff-necked people, forgive our wickedness and our sin, and take us as your inheritance."

Some points from this interaction between God and Moses can be applied to our own prayers of intercession. The first is Moses' heart. There were two desires that Moses cared about more than anything else. These two affections defined him. The first was God. Moses wanted nothing more than to obey God, fellowship with Him, and be in His presence. Moses was compelled by this desire to obey God even when he had no confidence in his own ability. He loved God, and communed with Him regularly. He desired God's presence more than His blessings.

The number one thing in Moses' heart was God, and the second was the people God had given him to lead. He loved these people so much that he went boldly before God for them over and over. He was even willing to die with them. Do we really care that much about the people God has placed in our lives? Do we even take the time to pray for them on a regular basis, much less have a willingness to die for them?

These people that Moses loved so much were not lovely. They were obstinate sinners who fiercely angered God. If we take the time to pray for others, is it for those in sin? Aren't we quicker to pray for those in need, the sweet innocent victims of the world who are afflicted in some way or another? Do we really pray in earnest for sinners?

What if these wretched sinners in our lives are Christians? The people Moses loved so much are more closely correlated to the Christians of today than any other group. They were God's people whom He had chosen and who had already seen His mighty power. This happens in our world all the time. God's people who know Him and are called by His name still commit awful sins. Unfortunately, all too often, the "Christian" reaction to such sinners is to push them away. We want to distance ourselves from them, implying through our separation that we are somehow different or better, instead of realizing that we are sinners too. Our fraudulent piety and lack of compassion is as big a sin as anything else, even though it may appear less colorful than other sins.

Does Moses' love for God and people remind you of anything? Moses' heart exemplified the words of Jesus in Matthew 22:37-40, "'Love the Lord your God with all your heart and with all your soul and with all your mind.' This is the first and greatest commandment.

And the second is like it: 'Love your neighbor as yourself.' All the Law and the Prophets hang on these two commandments.'" As prayer warriors, interceding for others, it is essential that we practice these two commandments, too.

Next, let's look at the content of what Moses said to God. Moses reminded God that He brought these people out of Egypt with His great power. Moses did not take the credit for bringing the people out. Instead, he correctly gave the credit to God. He asked God to turn away from His anger, even though that anger was deserved. Moses reminded God of His promises and added strength to his argument by further reminding God that He had sworn by Himself. In doing this, Moses approached God on God's terms, not his own. He petitioned God based on God Himself. Like Moses, we too can talk freely with God and remind Him of His promises found in His word.

Finally, Moses was persistent. He petitioned God numerous times with the same request. He repeatedly brought his case before God, based on God's own words and promises.

Moses intercedes even more

The book of Numbers records additional instances of Moses interceding for the children of Israel. In Numbers 11, the people complained because they wanted meat. They were wrong to grumble. They had manna provided by God, but they were not content with God's provision. They wanted their own way. They longed to eat meat. This time, Moses seemed exasperated. Their complaint burdened him. He knew this stubborn group of people was angering God yet again. He also knew that he had already stood between them and God's wrath many times, but they seemed not to have learned anything. In verses

PRAYER: IT'S NOT ABOUT YOU

11-12, he asked God, "What have I done to displease you that you put the burden of all these people on me? Did I conceive all these people? Did I give them birth? Why do you tell me to carry them in my arms, as a nurse carries an infant, to the land you promised on oath to their ancestors?"

This verse first caught my attention when a family friend struggled with a serious personal issue. At that particular time in my life, I was enjoying a period of peace after several turbulent years. The news of this person's problems shattered my peace. I found myself feeling as burdened for him as I would have been for my own child, and frankly, I did not like the feeling. I had been enjoying the sunshine of God's faithfulness in my life and I didn't want to enter into battle again, especially not for someone who was not a member of my family. I was happy to pray for this man from a safe distance, but I had no desire to intercede for him at this level of intensity or to feel this kind of pain on his behalf. It was emotionally exhausting, and I told God so.

For a while, I tried to convince myself this man's problems were not my burden. But I couldn't make the agonizing concern for him go away. Finally, one night as I began my devotions, this man came to my mind, and again I ached for him. In desperation, I asked God, "Why is this man my burden? He's not one of my kids. I have enough burdens of my own. Now don't put this man's burden on me, too. He is not my concern!" Then I opened my Bible to do my devotions.

There have been a few times in life when I have heard God speak so specifically to me that He might as well have been standing in the room speaking audibly. This was one of those times. That night I just happened to be reading in the book of Numbers in my devotions. I also just happened to be at chapter 11—and there it was on the page in front of me, the words I had just spoken to God. Moses also asked this same question to God, in almost the exact words. However, Moses was being asked to carry around the burden of over 600,000 people. I was only being asked to carry around one more—and yet, I complained about that. I laughed out loud when I read these verses and said, "Okay Lord, if Moses could carry around the burden of all those people, I guess I can carry around one more." Then I got with the program and started praying in earnest for the young man.

God answered Moses' plea in two ways. He had Moses gather some men to join him in leadership. God also told Moses that He would send meat to the people as they had asked. In Numbers 11:20, God said He would send so much meat that the people would have enough meat for a whole month until they loathed it.

Moses' response to this amuses me. A paraphrased version of what Moses said to God would go something like this, "With more than 600,000 people here, you say you will give them enough meat to eat for a month? What are you going to do, gather up all the fish in the sea? And even if you did, would it be enough?"

Proving once again that he was only human, Moses seemed to have forgotten that he was talking to God! This was the same God who appeared to him in a bush that burned, yet did not burn up. The God who sent masses of locusts, turned the waters into blood, killed all of the first born, parted the Red Sea, yet, Moses doubted God's ability to send enough meat to feed so many people. Aren't we just like Moses? We may have seen God work in marvelous ways in our lives, and the lives of those we love, but with every new challenge we still fear and doubt.

·God appeared a little fed up with Moses this time. He did not tell

Moses what He was going to do. Instead, in Numbers 11:23, He said, "Is the Lord's arm too short? Now, you shall see whether or not what I say will come true." In other words, God said, "Just wait and see!" Then, God sent a flock of quail that died suddenly right next to the Israelites' camp. And yes, there was enough meat to feed the people for a month. However, it did not feed them for a month, it made them sick—they indeed loathed it. Sometimes God gives us what we think we want; He allows us to have the wicked desires of our hearts in order to teach us to be happy with His provision without complaint.

In the twelfth chapter of Numbers, Moses made a different type of intercession. In this chapter, Miriam and Aaron, his sister and brother, grew discontented. They complained that Moses wasn't the only one God spoke through. They claimed God spoke through them, too. How did Moses react to this? Did he argue? Did he remind them that God spoke through him first? No, neither did he get angry or defensive. Instead, we read in verse three that he was a humble man, more humble than anyone else on earth.

Moses did not defend himself, but God did. God reminded Aaron and Miriam in Numbers 12:6-8, "When there is a prophet among you, I, the Lord, reveal myself to them in visions, I speak to them in dreams. But this is not true of my servant Moses; he is faithful in all my house. With him I speak face to face, clearly and not in riddles; he sees the form of the Lord. Why then were you not afraid to speak against my servant Moses?"

Then God struck Miriam with leprosy. Moses responded by pleading on Miriam's behalf. He did not revel in God's judgment against those who had spoken ill of him. Instead, in verse thirteen, he cried, "Please, God, heal her!" Do we do this? Jesus said we should. In

Mathew 5:44, Jesus said, "Love your enemies and pray for those who persecute you."

God granted Moses' request but He made Miriam suffer with leprosy for seven days first. Moses accepted God's answer without complaint. Numbers 12:15 tells us that Moses waited for his sister's full restoration before he moved forward. He was truly more concerned for the welfare of others than his own.

There they go again

Chapter Fourteen looks like a replay of events. God, Moses, and the Israelites are interacting the way they have so many times before. The people have heard a bad report from ten of the twelve spies. They are afraid, angry, and doubt God's ability to help them, again.

The people want to choose another leader and go back to Egypt—the land of their captivity. Again, they provoke God's anger, and again Moses intercedes. Picture the kind of man Moses was. The people wanted to get rid of him, God wanted to get rid of the people, and frankly, either option might have been easier than staying stuck in the middle between the two, being pulled both ways. But in the middle he stayed!

Have you ever been in those shoes? I have. I've had teenage children question my authority, other people outside our situation question my parenting skills, and I was stuck in the middle, walking beside, and praying for, my sometimes wayward children. All the while, I hoped they would not become so alienated from me, and the God I served, that they would never come back. Like Moses, almost any option seemed easier than standing beside, praying for, and trying to lead those teenagers who did not want to be led.

Moses again petitioned God based on God's own plan, His own promises, His character traits, and for His glory. We see this when Moses said in Numbers 14:13-19 (paraphrased), "If you destroy the people, what will the Egyptians think when they hear? They have heard that you, the true God are in the midst of these people. If you kill them, the Egyptians will say that you are not able to bring these people into the land you said you would give them." Moses reminded God that His name is at stake. He asked God to pardon the people for the glory of His own name. Moses also reminded God of the promise that He was slow to anger and abounded in steadfast love.

God again answered Moses' petition favorably while also allowing some consequences for the peoples' sins. He made them turn around and go back to the wilderness where they wandered for forty years until that generation died out. According to Numbers 14:28-31, when the children of Israel finally got to the Promised Land, none of the men who had grumbled were alive.

One of the most precious intercessions Moses made is recorded in Numbers 27:12-17. God let Moses see the Promised Land. However, according to Numbers 27:13-14, God told him he would not be allowed to enter the Promised Land. This was because Moses had rebelled at the waters of Meribah where he had failed to uphold God as holy before the eyes of the Israelites.

How do you think Moses reacted to the disappointing or even devastating news that he would never be allowed to enter the land he had spent most of his life in search of? Was Moses angry, sad, or filled with self pity? Did he defend himself before God? Hopefully, by now you know Moses well enough to know that he would not react in any of these ways. Remember, he was humble.

Moses knew God was both sovereign and just. Like always, Moses reacted with concern for the people. In Numbers 27:16-17 he asked God to appoint someone to lead the people in his place so the people would not be "like sheep without a shepherd." In His faithfulness, once again, God answered Moses' prayer telling him to appoint Joshua to lead the people. This is so precious! At a time when Moses experienced one of the greatest disappointments of his life, he was still more concerned with the needs of others than his own. I have to ask myself, am I like Moses? How often is my greatest concern the people God has put in my life to minister to and pray for, rather than myself? Not often enough, I'm afraid.

In studying Moses, we are studying one of the greatest intercessors in the Bible. He never defended himself against accusations, instead he prayed for his accusers. He had a human nature just as we do. He questioned God, but he never truly doubted Him. Although Moses frequently asked God, "*How* are you going to do that?" he never told God, "I don't think you *can* do that." He grew weary but he never quit, choosing instead to ask for help from God and others. He had no confidence in himself but complete confidence in his God. He communed with God often and obeyed Him always. Above all, he loved the Lord his God with all his heart, soul, and mind, and he loved his neighbor as himself. When he petitioned God, he did it not based on his needs or desires, but based on God's will, God's character, and for God's glory.

QUESTIONS FOR REFLECTION

Why did God choose Moses to be the intercessor for His people?

What two commandments did Moses exemplify?

Moses often doubted how God would do something and sometimes even argued with God, but what proved how much he loved God?

What can we learn about being a prayer warrior from Moses?

Chapter 3: David / the Psalms

David

Like Moses, David is one of the best-known characters in the Old Testament. Like the chapter on Moses, this book will look only briefly at David's life and more extensively at his prayers.

When Samuel, the priest, anointed David to become the next king of Israel, David was the least likely of Jesse's sons to be considered. So unlikely that according to the story found in 1 Samuel 16:1-13, Jesse did not even present him to Samuel for consideration. David was too young and insignificant. Samuel had to ask Jesse if he had any other sons before David was introduced to him.

God's plans are not our plans. They often do not fit our ideas of how things should go. Yet, they are always right, glorifying to God, and no matter how it might seem at any given moment, they are always good. My daughter expressed it well in a college philosophy paper when she wrote, "God's definition of good is different than man's definition. Man defines good as that which brings him a comfort of this life. God defines good as that which brings us closer to Him and into a life that is more glorifying to Him. God focuses on the eternal."[1]

What kind of man was David? What kind of man does God choose for His work? Like Moses, David was humble. He did not take credit for his successes but rightfully gave the credit to God. For example, in 1 Samuel 18:18-23, when King Saul offered to give David his daughter in marriage, David responded, "Who am I, and what is my family or clan in Israel, that I should become the king's son-in-law?" David said this even after Samuel had anointed him as the next king.

David experienced a period of brokenness. God's use of brokenness in the lives of His people is an interesting theme that runs throughout Scripture. Often before God uses a person, He first breaks him. In his book, *Laugh Again*, Charles Swindoll quotes Dr. Alan Redpath on this topic. Redpath said, "When God wants to do an impossible task, He takes an impossible man and crushes him."[2] Another Christian writer, A. W. Tozer wrote, "It is doubtful whether God can use a man greatly until He has first hurt him deeply."[3]

What seems confusing to Christians is the idea that God would bring about brokenness and pain in a person's life through the person's own failures or even sins, but this is often the case. God is not the author of sin. James 1:13 states this plainly, "When tempted, no one should say, 'God is tempting me.' God cannot be tempted by evil, nor does He tempt anyone." Nevertheless, we know from Romans 8:28 that God works through all things.

Through brokenness, even brought on by a person's own sins, God draws that person closer to Him. Like Moses experienced when he killed a man, and Peter experienced when he denied knowing Christ, David too experienced this type of brokenness. David lusted after Bathsheba, committed adultery with her, and then had her husband killed. Yet, consistent with God's promise to work good through all things, David wrote some of his most precious Psalms while in the state of brokenness that resulted from his sins. As we read these Psalms, we learn how to pray when we or those we love are broken by sin. These times of brokenness can be painful both for the one who is broken and for those who are standing close beside him or her. Rest assured, God is in it. If He were not, there would not be brokenness. The sinner would be content in his sinful state. That is a far worse condition!

David also suffered a protracted period of persecution by Saul. First Samuel 23:14 tells us that Saul sought him, trying to kill him, every day, but God did not give David into his hands. Persecution is another instrument God uses to mold His children and make them more dependent on Him. Genesis tells the story of Joseph—a slave and then a prisoner before he became second in command to the King of Egypt. From the Gospels we learn that the disciples were persecuted and tormented but grew bolder with each challenge. Even Jesus was beaten and nailed to a cross, died, and was buried, before He rose victoriously for all eternity. David experienced both persecution and brokenness. It is no wonder he was used by God in such a mighty way.

Finally, David was a man of faith. This faith can be seen many times in his life from his early encounter with Goliath until his old age. Unlike Moses, David never asked God how He was going to do something. David trusted God without question. One example of his unquestioning faith was David's willingness to fight Goliath. We will see this faith in greater depth as we look at his prayers.

David's Prayers

Most of what we know about David's prayers comes from the Psalms. Two prayers, however, are recorded elsewhere. The first of these is in 2 Samuel 12:7-18. This passage tells the story of the death of David and Bathsheba's first child. Nathan the prophet had confronted David concerning his sins of adultery with Bathsheba, and the murder of her husband. David repented, but even so, Nathan told him in verse fourteen that he would not die, but because of his sins, his child would.

Then, as prophesied, the baby became quite sick. While the baby was still alive, David petitioned God fervently for the child's life. David knew God's will. He knew the baby was going to die because Nathan had already said so. He petitioned God anyway. He fasted and lay on the ground all day and night for seven days. On the seventh day, the child died, just as God had said he would. After the baby died, David appears to have accepted God's answer as evident in 2 Samuel 12:16-20, which says that he arose, washed, anointed himself, and changed his clothes. Then he went into the house of the Lord to worship.

James 4:3 tells us, "When you ask, you do not receive, because you ask with wrong motives, that you may spend what you get on your pleasures." The King James Version calls this praying "amiss." The next chapter of James contains one of the greatest passages about prayer in all of Scripture.

"And the prayer offered in faith will make the sick person well; the Lord will raise them up. If they have sinned, they will be forgiven. Therefore confess your sins to each other and pray for each other so that you may be healed. The prayer of a righteous person is powerful and effective" (James 5:15-16).

This begs some questions. Was King David a righteous person? The answer is yes, he was righteous. Although he had sinned, he was again righteous before God because he had confessed his sins and received forgiveness. Did he not have enough faith? Certainly, he did have faith. His faith is precisely the reason he prayed so fervently. Why then was his petition not granted? The problem with his prayer and the reason his petition was not granted was that he was praying amiss. Simply stated, praying amiss is praying for things that are not in God's will, not in His plan. David already knew that his request was not

God's will because Nathan had told him that God had ordained for his baby to die. But David wanted his child to live so much, he prayed for it anyway. David was surely not too surprised when the baby died.

James identified praying amiss as praying for selfish gain, to use what one gets for his own pleasure. However, sometimes our amiss prayers do not appear to be selfish. Like David when he prayed for his baby to live, we can pray amiss in ways that may even appear benevolent. Nevertheless, anytime we pray in an attempt to get God to work according to our agenda, however benevolent that agenda may seem, instead of surrendering our will to His, we are praying amiss. Former missionary Susan Anderson wrote about her wrestle with this issue many years ago when she wrote, "There are some prayers that have not been granted, and I cannot understand why. A number of people would be much happier and better off in every way if the Lord could just see eye to eye with me and answer my prayers concerning them. So far, He has not and that is all I know about it. But I do not plan to give up trying to learn to pray."[4]

Sometimes we fall into thinking if we have enough faith, God will grant our petition. Faith is important in prayer but the focus needs to remain on God's plan, and not on our faith. If the measure of our faith is the focus, then if God does not grant our petition in the way we have asked, we falsely conclude that it is our own fault. We think we did not have enough faith instead of accepting "no" as God's answer. Likewise, if God grants our petition, guess who gets the glory? We do—for our great faith instead of God getting it for His great power. Romans 11:20 explains the attitude we should have regarding faith. It says, "… stand by faith. Do not be arrogant, but tremble."

When my parents were missionaries in Africa in the 1960's, they had the opportunity to observe pagans praying to their gods. The pagans practiced certain rituals and sacrifices to try to get their gods to answer their petitions. Their goal was to get their gods to do what they wanted. When Christians pray, we approach God seeking His will. Our goal is to get ourselves in line with His will so that we do what He wants. Our goal as Christians is just the opposite of the pagans' goal. Their goal was to get their god on their page; our goal is to get on God's page.

We can glean some points from David's amiss prayer. It's all right to pray whatever is on our hearts. We should feel comfortable enough in God's presence to pour our hearts out to Him. But we need to accept that sometimes God's answer is no. In addition, we learn that there are consequences for sins. David's baby died because of his sins. Finally, we need to remember that even when God's answer is no, we can still worship. David arose, washed, went into the House of the Lord, and worshiped. Then he broke his fast and ate.

Another of David's prayers that is not recorded in the Psalms can be found in 2 Samuel 7. In this chapter, David's heart was troubled because God did not have a house. So he decided to build a house for God. However, this was not God's plan. God told David by way of Nathan that he would not be allowed to build God's house. Instead, one of David's offspring would build it, a prophecy that was fulfilled later when David's son Solomon built the temple. But God also said that rather than David building Him a house, He was going to build David a house. God said He would raise up one of David's offspring and establish his throne forever. (This, of course, was fulfilled by Jesus, who was from David's line on both Mary and Joseph's sides.)

David responded by offering a prayer of gratitude. In his prayer, found in 2 Samuel 7:18-29, he included wording like, "Who am I, Sovereign Lord … that you brought me this far? … For the sake of your word and according to your will, you have done this great thing … How great you are, Sovereign Lord! There is no one like you and there is no God but you … And now, Lord God, keep forever the promise that you made … so that your name will be great forever."

Are we beginning to see a pattern, perhaps a method, for effective prayers? As we have seen before, and will see again, and again, David is essentially saying (paraphrased), "Lord, I pray this not because of me; I am nothing, but my prayer is because of You, for You are great. Because of Your promises and according to Your plans, You have done this. You did it for the sake of Your glory so that Your name will be glorified." David offered his prayer of thanksgiving in the same manner he petitioned God. In both cases, there was an awareness of God's greatness and of David's unworthiness. Both prayers were based on God's plan, because of His promises or character, and for His glory.

Then David added an interesting comment in verse twenty-seven when he said now that God had revealed this to him, he found the courage to pray about it What a fascinating verse! It reminds me of Elijah's prayer for rain when Elijah petitioned God for something he already knew had been promised. God had told David through Nathan that He was going to build him a house and establish his kingdom forever. Yet, instead of David saying something like, 'How nice, thank you," he told God that since God had revealed this to him, *he would have the courage* to ask for it in prayer.

Why did it take courage on David's part to ask God for what was already promised? Whenever we pray for God's will to be done, even at times when we clearly know how God is leading, there is a battle going on. This battle is in the spiritual realm against a real enemy who despises God, and desires to keep God's will from happening. This enemy despises us too, because we are made in God's image and are called by His name. So this enemy wants to attack us, accuse us, and ensnare us every chance he can. Whenever we engage in this battle through our prayers, it takes courage. David's prayer also reminds us of the importance of persistence even when we are praying about the things we believe God has already shown us.

The Psalms

"David composed many of them, the Israelites sang them, the church has recited them, and they all point to Jesus. Ultimately, they are all His songs."

Edward T. Welch

Depression a Stubborn Darkness[1]

If I were given the assignment to draw conclusions about prayer from a Biblical perspective, and was allowed the use of only one book of the Bible, I would choose the Psalms. Many of the Psalms are themselves prayers. A thorough study of these prayers will reveal several consistent themes, which can be divided into ten points.

Let's delve into them, paying special attention to Scriptures that relate to each.

1) Prayers are addressed to, or directed towards God, the Father.

Though this may seem obvious, some Christians are confused on this point. Some people pray to angels, to saints, to Mary the mother of

Jesus, or even to Jesus. Although there is scriptural precedent for praying to Jesus, for example, there are cases in the New Testament where people praised, thanked, or directed their petitions to Jesus while He was still here on earth, the vast majority of prayers in the whole of the Bible are directed to God the Father. Jesus Himself, when showing His disciples how to pray in Matthew 6:9 said, "This, then, is how you should pray: 'Our Father, in heaven …'"

Prayers should be prayed to the Father, through the Son, (or in the name of the Son) at the urging and with the help of the Holy Spirit. This dynamic will be explained more thoroughly in the New Testament section of this book. For now, we are only looking at evidence for this practice that can be found in the Psalms. The verses I have compiled are by no means a conclusive list.

4:1 "Answer me when I call to you, my righteous God … hear my prayer."

5:1 "Listen to my words, Lord …

30:8 "To you, Lord, I called; to the Lord I cried for mercy."

55:16 "As for me, I call to God, and the Lord saves me."

57:2 "I cry out to God Most High, to God, who vindicates me."

61:1 "Hear my cry, O God; listen to my prayer."

84:8 "Hear my prayer, Lord God Almighty."

102:1 "Hear my prayer, Lord; let my cry for help come to you."

123:1 "I lift up my eyes to you, to you who sit enthroned in heaven."

142:5 "I cry to you, Lord; I say 'You are my refuge, my portion in the land of the living.'"

2) Prayers contain praise and thanksgiving.

The Psalms are full of praise and thanksgiving. We will do well if our prayers are full, too. Everything we have, and every breath we take, is a gift from God. We owe Him much praise! We read many praise verses in the Psalms. One of my favorites is found in Psalm 69:30-31. "I will praise God's name in song and glorify him with thanksgiving. This will please the Lord."

At first glance, these look like any other verses that declare praises to God. What makes these verses unique is the context in which they are found. Psalm 69 is not a chapter where David praises God for all of His wonders or mighty works. Instead, it is a chapter where the writer is in great distress. He says things like, "Save me. O God!" and "I am worn out calling for help ... Those who hate me without reason outnumber the hairs of my head ... rescue me ... answer me .... I am scorned, disgraced and shamed ... scorn has broken my heart ..." Then, in Psalm 69:30-31, he writes, "I will praise God's name ... This will please the Lord." What makes this verse so powerful is that when taken in context, it brings tremendous clarity to certain aspects of praise.

- Praising God is a behavior we can choose, no matter how we feel.
- Praise is always appropriate, regardless of our circumstances.
- Praise to God is not based on our circumstances. Like other aspects of prayer, praise is about God and who He is, instead of us and how happy or comfortable we are.
- Praise pleases God.
- Praise is appropriate always and it is especially important when we are desperate for God to hear our prayers.

David's decision to praise God in spite of his circumstances revives his heart. He writes in verses 32-34 of Psalm 69, "…you who seek God, may your hearts live! The Lord hears the needy and does not despise his captive people. Let heaven and earth praise Him."

Below is a sample list of praise verses found in the Psalms:

7:17 "I will give thanks to the Lord because of his righteousness; I will sing the praises of the name of the Lord Most High."

9:1-2 "I will give thanks to you, Lord, with all my heart; I will tell of all your wonderful deeds … I will sing the praises of your name, O Most High."

18:3 "I called to the Lord, who is worthy of praise.

19:1 "The heavens declare the glory of God; the skies proclaim the work of his hands.

47:6 "Sing praises to God, sing praises …"

48:1 "Great is the Lord, and most worthy of praise."

67:3 "Let the peoples praise you, God, may all the people praise you."

113:3 "From the rising of the sun to the place where it sets, the name of the Lord is to be praised."

It is no coincidence that Psalm 150:6, the last verse in all of Psalms, says, "Let everything that has breath praise the Lord."

3) We should confess our sins and recognize our personal unworthiness.

I cannot stress enough the importance of recognizing our personal unworthiness and confessing our sins to God! Jesus made this point when he told the parable of the Pharisee and the tax collector who went to the temple to pray. The Pharisee stood in the temple where others could see him and boasted to God. Instead of confessing his sins, he claimed that he was not a sinner and he reminded God, in a loud voice so that everyone else around him could hear, that he fasted twice a week and tithed all that he earned. The tax collector did not even feel worthy to enter the temple or lift his eyes towards heaven. With downcast eyes, he admitted that he was a sinner and asked God for mercy. Jesus said this man's prayers were heard by God rather than the Pharisee's. Jesus added in Luke 18:14, "For all those who exalt themselves will be humbled, and those who humble themselves will be exalted."

If you do not remember anything else from this book, remember this: if you want your prayers to be heard by the one true, almighty, and holy God, you must humble yourself before Him.

This is not because God demands humility. Because of His steadfast love, God often exalts His children and lifts them to positions and tasks they never imagined they could do. *One humbles himself when he comes to God in prayer because it correctly reflects the truth of the situation. You and I really are nothing by comparison to Him and He is high and lifted up above all things both in heaven and on earth.* The following are some examples of this practice in the Psalms:

16:2 "Apart from you I have no good thing."

22:6 "But I am a worm and not a man…"

25:11 "Forgive my iniquity, though it is great."

38:18 "I confess my iniquity; I am troubled by my sin."

40:17 "But as for me, I am poor and needy."

51:3-4 "For I know my transgressions, and my sin is always before me. Against you, you only, have I sinned and done what is evil in your sight."

79:8 "May your mercy come quickly to meet us, for we are in desperate need."

86:1 "Hear me, Lord, and answer me, for I am poor and needy."

143:2 "No one living is righteous before you."

4) We can petition God based on His character.

This is the most difficult of all the points to write about simply because of the sheer volume of verses that pertain to it. To record all of these verses would require re-writing many of the Psalms. I have chosen, instead, to list many of God's character traits that are found in the Psalms, and give examples of the psalmist petitioning God based on them.

God's steadfast love

God's steadfast love is mentioned well over a hundred times in the Psalms, more than any other of God's traits. Of all God's many traits, the one He wants us to remember Him by most is His love—like so many of us learned as small children, "God is love" (1 John 4:8). Some of what the Psalms say about God's unchanging and steadfast love include:

It endures forever (Psalms 100:5, 107:1,118:1-4, 136:1-26, 138:8).

The Lord abounds in it (Psalms 86:15, 103:8, 145:8).

It is higher than the heavens (Psalms 57:10, 108:4).

The earth is full of it (Psalm 119:64).

It is from everlasting to everlasting (Psalm 103:17).

It is good (Psalms 69:16, 109:21).

It is better than life (Psalm 63:3).

It is priceless (Psalm 36:7).

It goes before God (Psalm 89:14).

He will crown us with it (Psalm 103:4).

He will keep it forever (Psalm 89:28).

He will not remove it (Psalm 89:33).

He takes pleasure in those who hope in His steadfast love (Psalm 147:11).

He shows it to us (Psalm 59:17).

He appoints it to protect us (Psalm 61:7).

He shows compassion because of it (Psalm 106:45).

Our responses to God's steadfast love should include:

We are to hope in it (Psalm 33:18).

We are to give thanks for it (Psalm 107:8, 15, 21, 31).

We sing of it (Psalm 59:16, 89:1).

We are to declare it (Psalm 89:2, 92:2).

We are to rejoice in it (Psalm 31:7).

We are to trust in it (Psalms 13:5, 52:8).

It comforts us (Psalm 119:76).

It holds us securely (Psalm 94:18).

Those who are wise will consider it (Psalm 107:43).

Through it we will enter God's house (Psalm 5:7).

Some of the ways in which David and the other Psalmists petitioned God appealing to, or based on His steadfast love are:

"In your unfailing love, silence my enemies" (Psalm 143:12).

"Deal with your servant according to your love" (Psalm 119: 124).

"In your unfailing love, preserve my life" (Psalm 119:88).

"Continue your love" (Psalm 36:10).

"Rise up and help us; rescue us for the sake of your unfailing love" (Psalm 44:26).

"Satisfy us … with your unfailing love" (Psalm 90:14).

"Save me in your unfailing love" (Psalm 31:16).

"In your great love, O God, answer me" (Psalm 69:13).

"Show us your unfailing love O Lord, and grant us your salvation" (Psalm 85:7).

"Have mercy on me, O God, according to your unfailing love" (Psalm 51:1).

Faithfulness

The character trait referred to in the Psalms the second greatest number of times is faithfulness. What the Psalms teaches about God's faithfulness includes:

All the paths of the Lord are loving and faithful towards those who keep the demands of his covenant (Psalm 25:10).

God abounds in faithfulness (Psalm 86:15).

Faithfulness surrounds God (Psalm 89:8).

It goes before God (Psalm 89:14).

God will not betray His faithfulness (Psalm 89:33).

It endures forever (Psalm 117:2).

It continually protects us (Psalm 40:11).

It is a shield (Psalm 91:4).

We walk in His faithfulness (Psalm 26:3 ESV).

The last is an interesting verse. In the English Standard Version, it says, "For your steadfast love is before my eyes, and I walk in your faithfulness." I have a friend who often says, "It's not that I walk faithfully with God, it's that God walks faithfully with me."[2]

God's trait of faithfulness is the basis of petitions in the following ways, as seen in these verses:

"Let evil recoil on those who slander me; in your faithfulness destroy them" (Psalm 54:5).

"In your faithfulness ... come to my relief" (Psalm 143:1).

"I know, Lord, that your laws are righteous, and that in faithfulness you have afflicted me" (Psalm 119:75).

This is by far the most intriguing verse on faithfulness. The New Revised Standard Version of the Bible says, "In your faithfulness, you have humbled me." Wow! Apparently, some of the times when we are afflicted or humbled, it is because of God's faithfulness to us. It seems paradoxical that God would afflict us in faithfulness. It is at least somewhat understandable for God to allow us to be afflicted as a consequence of our sins. However, I think there is more to it than that. In my life, when I have experienced afflictions or humbling, whether from my own sins or life circumstances, God has drawn closer to me and helped me. Always, He has produced through these times the fruits of righteousness and praise. These periods of affliction in our lives are not a result of God abandoning us, but rather because He is faithfully bringing us closer to Him and increasing our dependence on Him.

Fortress / Stronghold / Rock / Refuge

These characteristics of God are similar in nature. Numerous times the psalmist simply states as matter of fact that God *is* his refuge, fortress, stronghold, or rock (ex. 59:16-17, 46:1, 18:2, 31:3-4,144:1-2). At other times, the psalmist petitions God to *be* His refuge, fortress, stronghold, or rock as he does in Psalms 71:3 and 31:2.

At times David sounds like a lawyer arguing his case before a judge, based on the law. He will say for instance, "Be my rock of refuge, a strong fortress to save me" (31:2), while at the same time saying, "Since you are my rock and my fortress, for the sake of your name lead and guide me" (31:3).

You *are* a rock and fortress, so *be* a rock and fortress to me. Doesn't that sound like a lawyer? You can just hear a lawyer saying, "The law says such and such, now apply that law to my case."

David sees God's traits as a strong position on which to stand when petitioning God. This explains the concept of praying God's words back to Him. We learn who God is through reading and studying His word, then we can petition Him based on who He is—His character traits. Imagine going before a judge hoping for a favorable ruling. Would you feel more comfortable asking the judge to rule in your favor because of your wants and desires, or because there was a law that favored your position? Of course, you would rather petition a judge with the law on your side. You would be more confident of his ruling. It is a much stronger position.

The book of Psalms teaches us the following about God as a

stronghold, rock, refuge, and fortress:

Because God is our rock and fortress, we can take refuge in Him (18:2).

Because God is our stronghold, we do not need to fear (27:1).

Because He is our refuge, He is a help in time of need (37:39).

Because He is a rock and a fortress, we will not be shaken (62:2).

Because He is our rock, we can call upon Him (28:1).

God's people should remember that He is our rock (78:35).

Because He is our refuge, we can trust in Him and pour our hearts out to Him (62:7-8).

Shield

To say that God is a shield sounds similar to saying He is a rock, fortress, stronghold, or refuge. However, there is a subtle difference. A refuge and so forth provokes mental images of running to God as a safe haven, as if the person is hiding in God to escape the battle. A shield is used in the midst of battle to keep from being hit by oncoming artillery.

Sometimes the fact that God is a shield is simply stated as in the following passages: 7:10, 18:2, 33:20, 115:9-11, 144:2.

In addition, Psalms tells us:

God is a shield *around* us, not just in front of us (3:3).

He has given us the shield of His salvation (18:35).

He is a sun and a shield (84:11).

Our shield belongs to the Lord (89:18).

Help

The psalmist states both that God has been his help in the past (27:9, 30:2, 31:22) and that God is His help in the present and future (22:19, 33:20, 40:17, 70:5). In addition, we learn:

Our help is in the name of the Lord (124:8).

We are blessed when our help is God, and our hope comes from the Lord (146:5).

Based on the fact that God is his help, the psalmist petitions God to:

"Come quickly" (22:19) and to

"Hear my cry for mercy" (28:2).

Deliverer / Redeemer

Some of God's traits seem to make a progression. God is our refuge and fortress where we can hide from battle. He is our shield to stand firm in the battle. He is also our help when the enemy is overpowering us. And finally, He is our deliverer and redeemer. At times, He delivers us out of the battle and at other times, He redeems us from the enemy that has taken us captive.

Like with the other traits, the fact that God is our deliverer/ redeemer is simply stated as fact in some verses (18:2, 78:35, 144:2). In addition, God is sometimes petitioned on the basis of this trait, as in Psalm 70:5 where it says, "But as for me, I am poor and needy; come quickly to me, O God. You are my help and my deliverer; Lord, do not delay."

Goodness and Mercy

Because it is a fact that God is merciful (145:8, 86:15), God is petitioned to:

Remember the psalmist according to God's goodness, instead of remembering the psalmist's youthful sins (25:7).

Have mercy (51:1,123:3).

"In your great mercy, turn to me" (69:16).

We learn from Psalms that God's goodness or mercy is:

Is abundant (31:19,145:7).

Will satisfy us (65:4).

Is great (119:156).

We will dwell in it (68:10).

He crowns us with it (103:4).

He will not keep it from us (40:11).

Graciousness

Like the other character traits, this trait is also stated as fact (86:15, 116:5, 145:8), and yet used often as a basis for petitioning God. We see some of these petitions in the following verses:

"Be gracious to me for I am lonely and afflicted" (25:16).

"May God be gracious to us and bless us" (67:1).

"Be gracious to me according to your promise" (119:58).

Righteous / Upright / Holy

In contrast to all of the petitions offered to God based on His graciousness, mercy, steadfast love, and so many of His other traits, there is not a single petition in the book of Psalms based on the fact that God is righteous, upright, or holy. The reason for this is simple. God's holiness serves to point out our lack of holiness. Rather than petitioning God based on this trait, it reminds us of our personal unworthiness before God (Point #3). God's holiness forces us to confront our sinfulness, and realize that we can only be holy or righteous because of God's solution to our sin problem—Christ's blood shed for us on Calvary. Though never used as a basis for petitioning, the Psalms have a lot to say about God's holiness and how we should respond to it.

God is holy (99:3-5, 9).

His name is holy (30:4, 111:9).

His way is holy (77:13).

His promise is holy (105:42).

God is upright (25:8).

He is a righteous judge (7:11).

His promise is righteous (119:123).

His laws are righteous (119:7).

His statutes are righteous (119:144).

We should trust in His holy name (33:21).

We should praise His holy name (97:12).

Other Character Traits

The traits I have mentioned thus far are stated repeatedly in the Psalms. In addition, there are numerous other traits that are mentioned with less frequency. They are nonetheless part of God's character and can be used to petition Him when we pray. They include:

God is our portion (73:26, 119:57, 16:5, 142:5).

God is great and does marvelous things (86:10).

He alone is God (86:10).

He is slow to anger (145:8, 86:15).

He shows compassion (103:13).

He knows we are fragile, errant, humans. The NIV says He remembers we are dust (103:14).

He forgives our sins (103:3).

He heals diseases (103:3).

He rules, and before Him all shall bow (22:29).

He is the King of Glory, strong and mighty (24:8).

He is mighty in battle (24:8).

He is near to us (119:151).

All of His commandments are true (119:151).

He sees and hears (10:14, 10:17).

He encourages us (10:17).

He reigns. He is robed in majesty (93:1).

He does not sleep or slumber (121:4).

He is above all gods (135:5).

He sustains us (54:4).

He heals the brokenhearted (147:3).

He determines the number of stars (147:4).

He is mighty in power (147:5).

His understanding has no limit (147:5).

He sustains the humble (147:6).

He casts the wicked to the ground (147:6).

He delights in those who fear Him (147:11).

He grants peace (147:14).

He holds our hands (73:23).

He is the father to the fatherless and a defender of widows (68:5).

He is good (118:1).

He upholds the cause of the oppressed (146:7).

He gives food to the hungry (146:7).

He sets the prisoners free (146:7).

He opens the eyes of the blind (146:8).

He lifts up those who are bowed down (146:8).

He loves the righteous (146:8).

He lives (18:46).

His way is perfect (18:30).

His words are true (18:30).

His voice is powerful and full of majesty (29:4).

Even the darkness is not dark to Him (139:12).

He is our glory and the lifter of our heads (3:3).

He vindicates by His might (54:1).

5) We can petition God based on His promises.

Petitions based on God's promises are a clear basis for prayer found throughout the Scripture. However, it is not seen as often in the Psalms as in other places. Overwhelmingly, David's favorite means of petitioning God was on the basis of His character (Point #4). Even so, some of God's promises are referred to, or recorded in, the Psalms and are the basis of petitions in a few instances.

"Defend my cause and redeem me; preserve my life according to your promise" (119:154).

"Do not let me be put to shame ... No one who hopes in you will ever be put to shame" (25:2-3).

"Deliver me according to your promise" (119:170).

You and I can petition God based on any of His promises. I often search the Scriptures looking for promises that pertain to my given situation, in the same way a lawyer searches to find precedents that bolster his case.

6) We can petition God based on His ability to answer our prayer—asking Him to just do it!

Moses often petitioned God this way. Remember Exodus 34:9 where Moses asked, "Although this is a stiff-necked people, forgive our wickedness and our sin, and take us as your inheritance"? We see this type of prayer in the Psalms as well. These types of petitions are similar to point #7, petitioning God based on His sovereign will, and point #10, pouring our hearts out to Him. They are actually intertwined in that we often petition God this way when we know there is no hope for our situation other than God's divine intervention and mercy. We pour our hearts out to Him. We know that God's answer will only and always be according to His perfect will, God is always consistent with Himself. However, since it is often the case that we are confused as to what God's will is, it is nice to realize that we can petition Him for *anything*, remembering what Jesus said in Matthew 19:26, "With God all things are possible."

Passages in the Psalms where requests are made based on God's ability to answer or where the psalmist reminds himself of God's ultimate power and control include:

"Our God is in heaven; he does whatever pleases him" (115:3).

"But I trust in you, Lord; I say, 'You are my God.' My times are in your hands'" (31:14-15).

"You are the God who performs miracles; you display your power among the peoples" (77:14).

"It is God who judges: He brings one down, he exalts another" (75:7).

"How awesome are your deeds! So great is your power that your enemies cringe before you" (66:3).

"The God of Israel gives power and strength to his people" (68:35).

"Summon your power, God, show us your strength" (68:28).

"Arise, Lord, do not let mortals triumph" (9:19).

"Why do you hold back your hand ... Take it from the folds of your garment and destroy them!" (74:11).

7) We can petition God based on His sovereign will.

Petitioning God based on, and consistent with, His sovereign will forms the framework for all our other petitions. It puts everything else in the proper perspective. It also serves to keep us humble and submissive towards God. The psalmist's clear understanding of God's sovereignty is reflected in the following verses:

"The earth is the Lord's, and everything in it, the world, and all who live in it" (24:1).

"God rules forever by his power" (66:7).

"The Lord has sworn and will not change his mind" (110:4).

"Show me your ways, Lord teach me your paths" (25:4).

"You brought me from my mother's womb" (71:6).

"You know when I sit and when I rise; you perceive my thoughts from afar ... Before a word is on my tongue you, Lord, know it completely ... Where can I go from your Spirit? Where shall I flee from your presence? If I go up to the heavens, you are there; if I make my bed in the depths, you are there ... even there your hand shall guide me ... even the darkness will not be dark to you; ... For you created my inmost being ...Your eyes saw my unformed body; all the days ordained for me were written in your book before one of them came to be'' (139:1-16).

"The Lord reigns, let the nations tremble" (99:1).

8) We can petition God based on His own glory—for the sake of His own glory or for the sake of His name.

To glorify God is to demonstrate or draw attention to one of His traits. For example, if a wicked person turns to God and receives forgiveness, it is glorifying to God because it illustrates God's mercy and power to forgive sins. If he does not turn to God and receives just punishment, that is also glorifying because it draws attention to God's holiness, righteousness, and His rightful place as judge. This is why we cannot put God in our box. We cannot insist that He answer our prayers the way we want Him to because He may be glorified more to answer our prayers in a different way. Even so, we can petition Him to be glorified in the outcome and we can remind Him that we are His followers, trusting in Him, so the glory of His name is at stake in our prayers and in our lives.

As Christians, we should desire to glorify God in everything we do. A friend of mine struggled with depression at one point in his life. Through his struggle, he learned to depend on God and to lean on Him. My friend told me once about an experience he had while depressed and unable to sleep. On that particular night, when sleep would not come, he lay awake feeling sorry for himself. He cried out to the Lord all night in frustration and self pity asking, "Why? Why me? Why do I have to have depression and insomnia?" As he related this story to me, he sat back in his chair, crossed his arms, and said with a look of satisfaction on his face, "Then along about morning, I finally got my answer."

"What was your answer?' I asked, sitting on the edge of my seat.

He replied, in a matter of fact manner, "It doesn't matter. That's what God told me; it doesn't matter because it's not about me. If life was about me, then my questions would be valid, but it's not about me, it's about God. So it doesn't matter what He chooses to burden me with, I am to glorify Him, period!"

The psalmist too was aware of the significance of God's glory and often petitioned Him based on it, such as in the following verses:

"Not to us, Lord, not to us, but to your name be the glory" (115:1).

"Praise be to his glorious name forever; may the whole earth be filled with his glory" (72:19).

"Ascribe to the Lord the glory due his name; worship the Lord in the splendor of his holiness" (29:2).

"Be exalted, O God ... let your glory be over all the earth" (57:5).

"Yet he saved them for his name's sake, to make his mighty power known" (106:8).

"Some trust in chariots and some in horses, but we trust in the name of the Lord our God" (20:7).

"Help us, God our Savior, for the glory of your name" (79:9).

9) We should recognize what God has done in our lives— remembering His blessings and answered prayers, and thanking Him for them.

God is the creator of all things, the giver and sustainer of life. We do well to recognize the good things He has brought into our lives and thank Him. This pleases God. He does not demand it; He hears our prayers even when we forget to include thanksgiving. Nevertheless, we are remiss when we omit it. We do not want to be guilty of taking God's activity in our lives for granted. The writer of Psalms sets this example. Some of the verses that illustrate this include:

"We praise you, God, we ... tell of your wonderful deeds" (75:1).

"One generation commends your works to another; they tell of your mighty acts" (145:4).

"The Lord has done this, and it is marvelous in our eyes" (118:23).

"Come and see what God has done" (66:5).

"I called to you for help, and you healed me" (30:2).

"In you our ancestors put their trust ... and you delivered them" (22:4).

"We have heard with our ears, O God; our ancestors have told us what you did in their days" (44:1).

"I waited patiently for the Lord ... He lifted me out of the slimy pit, out of the mud and mire; he set my feet on a rock and gave me a firm place to stand" (40:1-2).

"I sought the Lord, and he answered me; he delivered me from all my fears" (34:4).

"He reached down from on high and took hold of me; he drew me out of deep waters. He rescued me from my powerful enemy, from my foes, who were too strong for me" (18:16-17).

10) We can pour out our hearts to God.

This last point is a sort of catchall. God wants us to share what is on our hearts with Him. We may have an intense burden on our hearts that does not seem to fit any of the other categories. What do we do in such cases? Where do we go when the burden is almost unbearable and we are confused? We take it to God. He is our Abba Father. He is our Daddy. He loves for us to turn to Him in difficult times. He is always there waiting to receive us and help us. (Remember His character traits. He is our comforter. His steadfast love is as high as the heavens and His faithfulness is firm.) Verses in the Psalms where this pouring out of the writer's heart is evident include:

"My God, my God, why have you forsaken me? ... My God, I cry out by day, but you do not answer, by night, but I find no rest" (22:1-2).

"Listen to my prayer, O God ... My thoughts trouble me and I am distraught" (55:1-2).

"I call with all my heart" (119:145).

"My tears have been my food day and night ... These things I remember as I pour out my soul" (42:3-4).

"I am worn out from my groaning. All night long I flood my bed with weeping and drench my couch with tears" (6:6).

"Turn to me and be gracious to me, for I am lonely and afflicted" (25:16).

"Evening, morning and noon I cry out in distress" (55:17).

"I pour out before him my complaint; before him I tell my trouble" (142:2).

"Trust in Him at all times ... pour out your hearts to him, for God is our refuge" (62:8).

These ten points can be seen numerous times in the Psalms. One example of how the psalmist incorporated these points can be found in Psalm 69. The passage quoted is from the English Standard Version of the Bible.

¹ Save me, O God! (#1 addressing our prayers to God)

   For the waters have come up to my neck.

² I sink in deep mire,

   Where there is no foothold ... (#10 pouring out our hearts)

³ I am weary with my crying out ... (#10 pouring out our hearts)

⁵ O God, you know my folly; the wrongs I have done are not hidden from you. (#3 recognizing our sins and unworthiness)

⁶ Let not those who hope in you be put to

   shame through me ... (#8 for the sake of God's glorious name.)

⁸ I have become a stranger to my brothers,

   an alien to my mother's sons ... (#10 pouring out our hearts)

¹³ But as for me, my prayer is to you, O Lord. (#1 addressing our prayers to God)

   At an acceptable time, O God, (#7 petitioning according to His will)

   in the abundance of your steadfast

love answer me in your saving faithfulness. [#4 petitioning based on God's character traits]

¹⁴ Deliver me from sinking in the mire … [#6 petitioning based on God's power and ability to do it.]

¹⁶ Answer me O Lord, for your steadfast love is good.

According to your abundant mercy, turn to me. [# 4 petitioning based on God's character traits]

¹⁷ Hide not your face from your servant;

for I am in distress … [#10 pouring out our hearts]

¹⁸ Draw near to my soul, redeem me … [#6 petitioning based on God's power a d ability to do it]

¹⁹ You know my reproach and my shame and my dishonor … [#3 recognizing our sins and unworthiness]

²⁰ Reproaches have broken my heart,

so that I am in despair … [#3 recognizing our sins and #10 pouring our hearts out]

²⁴ Pour out your indignation upon them,

and let your burning anger overtake them … [#6 petitioning based on God's power & ability to do it]

²⁶ For they persecute him who you have struck down,

and they recount the pain of those you have wounded … [#7 according to God's will]

²⁹ But I am afflicted and in pain;

let your salvation, O God set me on high! [#6 based on God's power]

³⁰ I will praise the name of God …

I will magnify Him with thanksgiving … [#2 praise & thanksgiving]

³³ For the Lord hears the needy and does not despise

his own people who are prisoners. [#5 based on God's promises]

³⁴ Let heaven and earth praise Him, [#2 praise & thanksgiving]

^{35} For God will save Zion. $^{(\#5\ based\ on\ His\ promises)}$

These ten points are repeated and reinforced throughout the Psalms. The content of our prayers should include these ten points. Whatever our requests, whether for ourselves or for others, our prayers should be directed to God from a heart that is humble and keenly aware of our own sins and unworthiness, filled with thanksgiving, praise, and petitions that are God-focused rather than self-focused. These petitions should be for His glory, because of His promises or character, and for the purpose of fulfilling His sovereign will.

I cannot close this chapter without passing on my favorite verse about prayer. Actually, it is hard to claim a favorite because I have so many, but this verse is certainly the one I remember the best. It is Psalm 109:4, "But I am a man of prayer." That isn't even a whole verse, it is just a part of a verse—just seven words, but it says it all. What makes this verse so powerful is the context in which it appears. In the verses that precede it, David complained adamantly about his situation. He begged God not to be silent, telling God that he was being treated unfairly. People were lying about him. They encircled him with hate, they attacked him without cause. In return for his love, they accused him. They rewarded him evil for good, and hatred for love. Then, after saying all of this, David wrote "but I am a man of prayer."

David was a mighty soldier with a strong army of men who would fight for him at his command. David was a king. Yet, in response to these wicked opponents, he did not say that he would wage war against them, issue decrees against them, or have them killed or imprisoned. No, David's choice of action against the strong and wicked forces that opposed him was the same choice you and I can make in whatever frightening or difficult circumstances we find ourselves. It seems that in David's mind, the strongest weapon he had against his enemies was prayer. Like David, in our times of trouble, we too can cry, "But I am a man (or woman) of prayer!"

QUESTIONS FOR REFLECTION

What does it mean to pray amiss? When did David pray amiss?

Name the guidelines for the content of our prayers.

Chapter 4: Hannah, Samuel, Daniel, Nehemiah, Ezra, and Habakkuk

We can read and learn from the prayers of several more Old Testament characters. In the following chapters, we'll look at Hannah and Samuel, Daniel, Nehemiah, Ezra, Habakkuk, Abraham, Jacob, Hezekiah, Solomon, Jehoshaphat, and Job.

Hannah

In the first and second chapters of 1 Samuel, we find the story of Hannah's prayer for a child. Although Hannah prayed for her yet-to-be-conceived son, she also prayed for herself. She was praying about her own needs and deepest desires. She desperately wanted a child so she turned to God knowing that only He could grant this petition, and give her this desire of her heart.

Hannah wanted to conceive. She prayed earnestly for a child, so earnestly Eli the priest thought she was drunk. He could see her lips moving but no sound came from her voice because she was praying in her heart. Assuming her to be drunk, Eli scolded her but she explained that she was not drunk, she was pouring her heart out to God because of her intense desire to have a child.

God is pleased when we pour our hearts to Him. Sometimes He even brings us to the point of agonizing in prayer, like He did Hannah, so we will do just that. Psalm 62:8 tells us to "Trust in him at all times … pour out your heart to Him, for God is our refuge." Lamentations

2:19 says, "Pour out your heart like water in the presence of the Lord. Lift up your hands to him for the lives of your children." Isaiah 26:16 says, "Lord, they came to you in their distress when you disciplined them, they could barely whisper a prayer."

God answered Hannah's prayer. He gave her a son whom she named Samuel. In 1 Samuel 1:27 we read Hannah's famous words, "I prayed for this child, and the Lord has granted me what I asked of him." Then in chapter 2, after Samuel was born, Hannah prayed a beautiful prayer of thanksgiving and praise.

Samuel was called by God as a priest, judge, and prophet. He was used of God to intercede for, and to guide God's people. He anointed David as king over Israel. Was all of this an afterthought on God's part in response to Hannah's prayer? In other words, do our prayers change God's plans? Certainly not. Hebrews 4:3 tells us "his works have been finished since the creation of the world." Psalm 33:11 says, "But the plans of the Lord stand firm forever." Revelation 17:8 speaks of people "whose names have not been written in the book of life from the creation of the world." If Samuel's name was written in the Lamb's Book of Life from the creation of the world, then we can safely say that his birth was not a change in God's plan made in response to his mother's prayers.

Rather, it is likely that Hannah's desire for a child was laid on her heart by God, and her earnest prayer was part of the unfolding of God's amazing plan. The intriguing question remains then, why was Hannah distressed and vexed to the point of pouring her heart out to God with such fervor that she appeared drunk? Ahh, the mystery of prayer!

Again, we see a situation not unlike that of Elijah praying so earnestly for the rain that God had already told him was coming.

Mysteries are by definition hard to comprehend. Personally, I think God laid this request on Hannah's heart with such heaviness in order to cause her to pray so fervently. He knew she was a trustworthy servant with the burden He had given her. He knew that she would turn towards Him instead of turning away from Him. One lesson we can learn from this is that when we see our prayers answered, instead of it being proof that God is listening to us, it should be seen as evidence that we are listening to God, and are in tune with His will.

I'm glad God included Hannah's prayer in Scripture. It is nice to know that we can talk to God about our own personal pain, needs, and desires. Hannah was deeply distressed. She prayed to the Lord and wept bitterly. She made a vow to God that if He gave her a child, she would give the child back to Him. She remembered her vow. First Samuel 1:10-24 tells us that when he was old enough, she brought him to the temple to live.

I am not an advocate of bargaining with God. Requests should be made with an attitude of complete submission and reverence. We can pray fervently, fiercely, and continually, but seldom would bargaining be appropriate. Hannah's case was one of the few exceptions. As Samuel's story unfolds, it is evident that God's plan was indeed for Hannah to give Samuel back to Him. It appears that even this bargaining on the part of Hannah was orchestrated by God for bringing about His purposes for Samuel, and for the nation of Israel. In other similar instances in Scripture, God also initiates someone's prayer. He places the request or desire into the heart of the one making it for the purpose of fulfilling His will. One example of this is Ezekiel 36:37-38 (ESV), where God says, "This also I will let the house of Israel ask me to do for them, to increase their people like a flock ... so shall the waste cities be filled with flocks of people. Then they will know that I am Lord."

Finding God's will can be like reading a treasure map. We did not make the map, nor plant the treasure; likewise, we should not plan our lives or seek our own rewards. Instead, we search eagerly in our effort to follow the map that God has made for us. It is an adventure like none other, a mystery that unfolds around us. Prayer is a part of that adventure. We learn to be sensitive to God's leading. When we have a desire in our hearts, we can take it to the Lord in prayer, seeking to know if it is from Him. Then we can move forward in our lives as the Lord opens some doors to us while also closing others.

Samuel

The stage was set for Samuel to become the new priest when in 1 Samuel 2:12-13 God rejected the sons of Eli because of their sins. Chapter 3 records the well known and precious story of God calling Samuel into His service while he was still a young child.

You may remember this story. According to 1 Samuel 1:11-3:9, Samuel lived at the temple with Eli, the priest. One night he heard God's audible voice calling him. Because he had never heard God before, he mistakenly thought the voice belonged to Eli. Samuel arose from his bed and went to Eli to see why he called. Samuel did this several times until Eli, realizing that it must be God's voice, told the child to go back to his bed and respond with, "Speak Lord, for your servant is listening."

By Chapter 7, we find Samuel a grown man. He told the people to gather at Mizpah and he would pray for them. This prayer for the people occurred after Eli and his sons had been killed and Israel had been defeated in battle by the Philistines. The Israelites were a humble group at this point in time. First Samuel 7:6 says they gathered at Mizpah, fasted, and said, "We have sinned against the Lord." Often people turn to God when they are defeated and discouraged. Sometimes God allows problems for this very reason. The people asked Samuel to never stop praying for them.

A few points may be gleaned or reiterated from Samuel's prayer for the people. The people approached God with an awareness of their unworthiness. They were conscious of their sins and wanted forgiveness. They also asked Samuel to pray for them *continually*. Likewise, 1 Thessalonians 5:17 tells us to pray continually. Isaiah 62:6-7 says, "You who call on the Lord, give yourself no rest, and give him no rest ..."

Samuel's awareness of this truth can be seen in his response to the people's request for prayer. In 1 Samuel 12:23, he said, to the people, "As for me, far be it from me that I should sin against the Lord by failing to pray for you." 1 Samuel 7:13 adds that the "throughout Samuel's lifetime, the hand of the Lord was against the Philistines." No doubt there's a connection between the fact that Samuel did not cease praying for the people and God's hand being continually against their enemy all of his days.

1 Samuel 8 tells that when Samuel was old, he made his sons judges over Israel. However, his sons did not live in a way that honored God. They took bribes and perverted justice.

So, the people begged for a king. God told Samuel to listen to the voice of the people and anoint a king over them. Then, God had Samuel anoint Saul as their king. Saul proved to be a king who did not follow after God with his whole heart. Samuel must have had times when he questioned why God had told him to anoint Saul. In 1 Samuel 15:10-11 the word of the Lord came to Samuel saying, "'I regret that I have made Saul king, because he has turned away from me ...' Samuel was angry, and he cried out to the Lord all that night."

The Scriptures do not let us know whether Samuel was angry with himself, with Saul, or with God when he cried out to God all night long. But this much is clear, being an active part of God's plan was no small thing to Samuel. He agonized over God's condemnation of King Saul and like his mother Hannah, he poured out his heart to God. Nevertheless, in 1 Samuel 15:12, he rose early the next morning to meet with Saul in obedience to God.

I have been impressed in my study of Scripture by how many of God's people "rose early" to do whatever it was they knew God wanted them to do. In Genesis 21-22, we see this several times. Abraham rose early to send Hagar and Ishmael away even though he loved Ishmael. He rose early again to take his son Isaac to offer as a sacrifice to God. This was not something he was eager to do, but he knew God had told him to do it so he "rose early" and obeyed. Jacob rose early after his dream, took the stone he had been lying on, and made it an altar to God. In Joshua 6:12, Joshua rose up early and brought Israel by tribes. And on and on it goes. In many of these cases, the tasks these followers of God faced were not pleasant, but because they were certain of what God wanted them to do, they rose early even if they had wrestled with the issue all night like Samuel.

When Samuel told Saul that God had rejected him and was going to take the kingdom away, Saul appeared remorseful. In 1 Samuel 15:25, he said, "Now I beg you, forgive my sin and come back with me, so that I may worship the Lord." Saul continued in verse 30 saying,

"I have sinned. But please honor me before the elders of my people and before Israel; come back with me, so that I may worship the Lord your God." Although Saul seemed to admit his sin, if we look carefully, we see that he did not ask Samuel to pray for him, nor did he seek God's forgiveness. Instead, Saul asked for Samuel's forgiveness immediately followed by a request that Samuel honor him before the elders and all of Israel by making an appearance with him. Saul was apparently still much more concerned with what people thought than with what God thought.

Later, in verse 35, we learn that Samuel did not see Saul again until the day of his death, but Samuel grieved over Saul. We get a glimpse into Samuel's heart in this verse. He was personally saddened by the turn of events but he knew it was God's will.

He was obedient to God's commands even though it pained him. God then told Samuel to anoint David as the next king in 1 Samuel 16:7, where God said, "Do not consider his appearance or his height ... The Lord does not look at the things people look at. People look at the outward appearance, but the Lord looks at the heart."

Samuel's life was an answer to his mother's heartfelt prayer. He lived his life as a man of prayer who had God's hand upon him. I love studying Hannah and Samuel. From Hannah we learn to pour our hearts to God. From Samuel we learn to obey God even when we do not like what He has told us to do. And from both we learn that God is real, He hears our prayers, and He answers when we pray.

Daniel

Daniel's prayer of intercession for his people is recorded in the ninth chapter of the book of Daniel. He studied Jeremiah's prophecy concerning Jerusalem and became aware of God's plan, causing him to turn to God in prayer to petition Him according to that plan. Once again, we can draw a correlation to Elijah's prayer for the promised rain. God has a plan, and He lays it on our hearts to pray for it. It is His plan, His work for His creation. Yet He invites us to participate in the work with Him. Our prayers are useful to God and part of His method for bringing about His will.

In Daniel 9:3, he writes, "So I turned to the Lord God and pleaded with him in prayer and petition, in fasting, and in sackcloth, and ashes." His prayer, recorded in Daniel 9:4-18, is a great example of how we should pray on behalf of others. Here is his prayer:

"Lord, the great and awesome God, who keeps his covenant of love with those who love him and keep His commandments … We have been wicked and have rebelled; we have turned away from your commands and laws … Lord you are righteous but … we are covered with shame …

Now, Lord our God, who brought your people out of Egypt with a mighty hand, and have made for yourself a name … we have sinned, we have done wrong. Lord, in keeping with all your righteous acts, turn away your anger and your wrath from Jerusalem, your city, your holy hill …

Now, our God, listen to the prayers and petitions of your servant. For your sake, Lord, look with favor on your desolate sanctuary. Give ear, our God, and hear; open your eyes and see the desolation of the city that bears your Name. We do not make requests of you because we are righteousness, but because of your mercy."

Are similarities becoming apparent in the various prayers recorded in Scripture? Certainly, comparisons can be made between this prayer and others. Like Elijah, Daniel petitioned God to do what God had already said He would do. The content of Daniel's prayer is quite similar to David's prayers. They both confess the sins of the people, and acknowledge corporate unworthiness. Daniel said, "We are covered with shame," in one of the Bible's best example of humility in prayer. Daniel said that God has righteousness, mercy, and forgiveness, but he and his people were covered in shame.

Also like David, Daniel remembered the works God had done, while again confessing his and his people's sins. Then, he petitioned God to turn His anger away for God's own sake, for the sake of God's name. Daniel re-stated in verse 18 that his pleas were based on God's traits of mercy not on his or his people's righteousness. Then he petitioned once again for God to hear, forgive, pay attention, and act for God's own sake because the city and people were called by God's name. Like David, Daniel prayed according to God's will and for the sake of God's name. And like Hannah, Daniel poured out his heart to God.

Nehemiah

Nehemiah's prayer, which is recorded in Nehemiah 1:4-11, sounds a lot like Daniel's prayer. In verses 1-3 of this passage, we see what prompted Nehemiah to pray. He had inquired as to the wellbeing of the Jews who had escaped and survived the exile, as well as the condition of the city of Jerusalem. He received discouraging news. The exiles were in great peril and shame, the wall of Jerusalem was broken down, and its gates had been destroyed by fire.

This report distressed Nehemiah greatly. In Nehemiah 1:4 he wrote, "When I heard these things, I sat down and wept. For some days I mourned and fasted and prayed before the God of heaven." This sounds so much like Daniel 9:3 where Daniel turned his face to the Lord God and sought Him by prayer with fasting, sack cloth, and ashes. James 5:16 in the King James Version says, "The effectual fervent prayer of a righteous man availeth much." Fervent prayers of righteous men are exactly what we see with Daniel and Nehemiah. These were men willing to stand in the gap for others. The concept of standing in the gap for someone is derived from Ezekiel 22:30 where God said, "I looked for someone among them who would build up the wall and stand before me in the gap on behalf of the land."

I have a friend who says that she sometimes thinks that she would rather not know of all the trouble others around her are in because it distresses her so. It would be easier to ignore these needs and assume all is well. But invariably, God opens her eyes to the pain around her. She has finally come to realize that God's purpose is not to distress her, but rather so she will know what to pray. She once said, "I have come to realize that my goal in life is to wake up one morning with everything going so well that I have nothing to pray for. But that is clearly not God's goal for me. He keeps showing me awful and seemingly hopeless situations that I need to pray about."[1]

My friend is a prayer warrior. God knows she will stand in the gap for others so He keeps calling her to duty. But it is a difficult and often painful task. Daniel fasted, prayed, and wore sackcloth and ashes because he was in such distress. Nehemiah sat down and wept and mourned for days before he began praying and fasting. Are we getting the picture? Intercessory prayer is hard work. Emotionally and spiritually draining, intercessory prayer is a weapon we use in a real and difficult battle. We are called to fight with boldness. To quote another friend, "We should engage in battle fiercely, instead of just sitting around twirling our swords of the Spirit in the air." [2]

The content of Nehemiah's prayer as recorded in Nehemiah 1:5-11 is as follows:

"Lord, the God of heaven, the great and awesome God, who keeps his covenant of love with those who love him and keep His commandments ..." (Did you notice these are almost the exact words Daniel used when he began his prayer?)

"Let your ear be attentive and your eyes open to hear the prayer your servant is praying before you day and night." (Again, this is similar to Daniel 9:18 where Daniel asked God to incline His ears and open His eyes.)

"I confess the sins we Israelites, including myself and my father's family, have committed against you ... They are your servants and your people, whom you have redeemed by your great strength and your mighty hand. Lord, let your ear be attentive to the prayer of this your servant and to the prayer of your servants who delight in revering your name. Give your servant success today."

Nehemiah is so greatly distressed by the situation that like Hannah, he poured out his heart to God. Like Samuel, he did not cease praying. Nehemiah 1:6 says he prayed both day and night. Like David and Daniel, he directed his prayers to God, confessing his sins and the sins of his people. Like Moses, he reminded God that these were God's people whom He had redeemed by His power and strong hand. And like them all, he asked God to grant his petition for God's own glory.

Ezra

Scripture records two of Ezra's prayers. The first of these can be found in the ninth chapter of Ezra. Ezra had just learned that God's people had sinned by intermarrying. God had commanded the Israelites at this time in history not to intermarry with the people around them. This was not a statement against inter-racial marriage. The purpose of this command was to preserve their faith. Intermarrying would have caused the children of Israel to embrace the beliefs of the people whom they married and to begin worshiping other gods—and that is exactly what happened. By intermarrying with the non-Jews around them, the Israelites acted contrary to God's specific orders. Ezra's reaction to the news of their sin is recorded in Ezra 9:3-4 where he writes:

"When I heard this, I tore my tunic and my cloak, and pulled hair from my head and beard and sat down appalled. Then everyone who trembled at the words of the God of Israel gathered around me because of the faithlessness of the exiles. And I sat there appalled until the evening sacrifice."

I don't mean to be irreverent, but I find the passage a little funny. It conjures up a mental image of Ezra sitting speechless with his jaw nearly touching the ground for hours and hours. When I first discovered this passage, the version I read said Ezra "sat appalled." I shared it with one of my friends. I told her that I was not sure what exactly it meant to sit appalled. She replied, "Me either, but I think I've been there."[1]

Well, however it was that Ezra sat when he was appalled, it

certainly indicates his recognition of the gravity of sin. Because we live on this side of the cross, in the age of grace, we often forget just how ugly sin really is. Those who lived in the Old Testament times had a better understanding of the gravity of sin. Daniel said the people were covered with shame, Nehemiah wept and mourned for days, Ezra sat appalled, and they all fasted and prayed.

Sin is that bad. We should all sit appalled at our own sins and admit with the apostle Paul in 1 Timothy 1:15, that we too are the chief of sinners. Paul said this towards the end of his ministry after having evangelized the entire known world, and after having written many of the books of the New Testament. Why did Paul call himself the chief of sinners? Did he say it because he *actually* sinned more at the end of his ministry? No, I don't think so. Rather, perhaps he said this at that time in his life because as he had grown in his walk with the Lord, he had gained a greater ability to recognize his own sinful nature.

When praying for ourselves or for others, we need to understand the gravity of sin. Our understanding of God and His greatness directly correlates to our ability to recognize the ugliness of sin and how sin separates us from God. Our ability to recognize sin influences our ability to see our own personal unworthiness, which is necessary in order to come before God with the proper attitude.

Ezra 9:5-13 tells us that at the time of the evening sacrifice, Ezra rose from his fasting, fell to his knees, and spread out his hands to the Lord. Then he prayed:

"I am too ashamed and disgraced, my God, to lift up my face to you, because our sins are higher than our heads and our guilt has reached to the heavens ... But now for a brief moment, the Lord our

God has been gracious in leaving us a remnant ... Though we are slaves, our God has not forsaken us in our bondage ... But now, our God, what can we say?

... and yet, our God, you have punished us less than our sins deserved ... Shall we then break your commands again and intermarry with the peoples who commit such detestable practices? Would you not be angry enough with us to destroy us, leaving us no remnant or survivor? ... Here we are before you in our guilt, though because of it not one can stand in your presence."

Then Ezra 10:1 goes on to describe Ezra's bodily position while he prayed. He cast himself down before the house of God.

Ezra's other prayer is recorded in Ezra 8:21-23.

"There, by the Ahava Canal, I proclaimed a fast, so that we might humble ourselves before our God and ask him for a safe journey for us and our children, with all our possessions. I was ashamed to ask the king for soldiers and horsemen to protect us from enemies on the road, because we had told the king, 'The gracious hand of our God is on everyone who looks to him, but his anger is against all who forsake him.' So we fasted and petitioned our God about this, and he answered our prayer."

This prayer is a good summary of all that we usually pray for and the reason we pray. We pray for "safe journey" through life for ourselves, our children, and our possessions. And the reason we pray is for His namesake, because we are His followers, and like Ezra, we believe His hand is gracious towards all who look to Him.

I am especially fond of this prayer because it shows that we can freely pray about tangible, physical needs. Although it is important to focus on spiritual things, it is comforting to realize that, like Ezra, we can ask God to watch over us, our children, and our possessions.

Habakkuk

Habakkuk's prayer can be found in chapter three of the book of Habakkuk. This prayer is a little different from others we have studied, in that Habakkuk is not interceding on behalf of his people. His prayer reads more like a personal conversation with God. He begins in verse two, by saying, "Lord, I have heard of your fame; I stand in awe of your deeds, Lord. Repeat them in our day, in our time make them known; in wrath remember mercy." In this opening sentence, Habakkuk does so many of the things we have seen before. He addresses his prayers to God, focuses his thoughts on God, acknowledges his insignificance in comparison to God, and petitions for mercy—one of God's character traits.

Then, in verses 3-15, Habakkuk reviewed Israel's history and God's work in that history. Habakkuk believed that because God worked in the past, He could be trusted with the future. In verse 16, he admitted his fear regarding a prophetic vision he had about Israel's future. He wrote, "I heard and my heart pounded, my lips quivered at the sound; decay crept into my bones, and my legs trembled. Yet I will wait patiently for the day of calamity to come on the nation invading us."

But Habakkuk determined in his heart that he will accept from the hand of God whatever God brought, knowing that no matter how frightened he was, or how unpleasant the fulfillment of the vision might be, God would be acting according to His sovereign will. Therefore, with complete trust in God, Habakkuk chose to praise Him. Evidence of his choice to praise God can be found in verses 17-19 of chapter 3. These are wonderful verses in which Habakkuk rejoiced in the Lord in spite of his circumstances or fear. He wrote:

"Though the fig tree does not bud and there are no grapes on the vines, though the olive crop fails and the fields produce no food, though there are no sheep in the pen and no cattle in the stalls, yet I will rejoice in the Lord, I will be joyful in God my Savior. The sovereign Lord is my strength; he has made my feet like the feet of a deer, he enables me to tread on the heights. "

From Habakkuk's prayer we learn to pray in line with God's will, and to accept it, no matter how it affects us. We are also reminded once again that praising God is a choice we can make regardless of our circumstances.

QUESTIONS FOR REFLECTION

Hannah and Samuel

What important lesson about prayer do we learn from Hannah?

If our prayers are answered favorably, what does this indicate about our understanding of God's plan?

Daniel, Nehemiah, and Ezra

What similarities can be drawn between the prayers of Daniel, Nehemiah, and Ezra and the other prayers that we have seen in so far in the book?

What specifically did Daniel, Nehemiah, and Ezra do or say that indicated their earnestness as well as recognition of their needy state?

Habakkuk

What do we learn from Habakkuk's prayer?

Chapter 5: Abraham, Jacob, Hezekiah, Solomon, and Jehoshaphat

Abraham

The Bible records many conversations between Abraham and God, but the one we'll focus on now is found in Genesis 18:23-32. In this passage, God had just told Abraham that He was going to destroy the wicked cities of Sodom and Gomorrah. Abraham was alarmed by this news because his nephew, Lot, lived in Sodom as well as Lot's family. The English Standard Version quotes Genesis 18:23-25 as saying:

"Then Abraham drew near and said, 'Will you indeed sweep away the righteous with the wicked? Suppose there are fifty righteous within the city, will you ... not spare it for the fifty righteous who are in it? ... Shall not the judge of all the earth do what is just?'"

As we read this request made by Abraham to God, it should be noted that Abraham's petitions were in line with God's character. Abraham also *drew near to God* when he petitioned Him. In response to his request, God agreed to spare Sodom if He found fifty righteous people.

Abraham pushed his request a little further asking if God would spare the city if there were only forty-five righteous people in it. Again God agreed to spare the city for the sake of the forty-five. Abraham continued petitioning in Genesis 18:30-33 until he had God agreeing to spare the city for the sake of only ten righteous people. Each time Abraham made his request, he was aware of his own unworthiness before God as indicated by comments like, "I am but dust," and "Oh let not the Lord be angry." Each time God agreed to spare the city per Abraham's request. Then after agreeing to spare the city for the sake of only ten righteous people, God went His way.

We know from further reading that there were not even ten righteous people in the city of Sodom. In all of Sodom and Gomorrah the only righteous person was Abraham's nephew Lot. Genesis 19:29 tells us, "So when God destroyed the cities of the plain, he remembered Abraham, and he brought Lot out of the catastrophe that overthrew the cities where Lot had lived." God did not spare the city. However, because of Abraham's petitions, He spared Lot. God did not let the righteous perish with the wicked.

Genesis 19:27-28 tells us that on the morning the cities were destroyed, Abraham went back to the place where he had stood before the Lord. He looked down toward Sodom and Gomorrah and saw the smoke from the burning cities—what a poignant scene. Abraham must have been saddened by the knowledge there were not even ten righteous people in the city. It is also likely that he did not know, at that time, whether his nephew had been saved. He probably had feelings of fear and dread. Yet consider where he was at this difficult time in his life. He was back at the place where he had previously met with God— the place where Abraham had previously *drawn near to God.* I think there is a lesson for us in that.

In Abraham's prayer, we see his humility and his obvious awareness of who he was in comparison to God. Yet, in spite of his human frailties, Abraham boldly made his request to God. These requests were consistent with God's ability to protect His own. We also see from Abraham's prayer the practice of being persistent in our petitions, and the fact that God answers the prayers of His people. Finally, we see in this exchange the lesson of going back to the place where we previously met with God when our circumstances are challenging.

Jacob

Jacob's prayer can be found in Genesis 32:9-12. At the time of this prayer, Jacob was afraid. He was about to meet his brother Esau whom he had not seen in many years, and from whom he had fled in fear.

Growing up, Jacob had been their mother's favorite child while Esau had been their father's favorite. Parenting with favoritism toward one child over another always fosters ill will between siblings. In addition, Jacob had stolen Esau's birthright and tricked him out of his blessing. Esau hated Jacob and determined to kill him after their father died. Because of this threat, their mother Rebecca sent Jacob away so that he would be safely out of danger.

The prayer recorded in Genesis 32 occurred many years later, after Jacob was a wealthy man with wives and children. Esau had become wealthy, too, and was able to attack Jacob if he so chose. Jacob was frightened. He feared for his life and for the lives of his family. Yet he was able to draw strength from his memory of God's promises to him. Here is Jacob's prayer, found in Genesis 32:9-12:

"O God of my father Abraham, God of my father Isaac, Lord, you said to me, 'Go back to your country and your relatives, and I will make you prosper,' I am unworthy of all the kindness and faithfulness you have shown your servant. I had only my staff when I crossed this Jordon, but now I have become two camps. Save me, I pray, from the hand of my brother … for I am afraid he will come and attack me, and also the mothers with their children. But you have said, 'I will surely make you prosper and will make your descendants like the sand of the sea, which cannot be counted.'"

As we dissect this prayer, we see again some of the same themes that have appeared in the other prayers we have studied. Jacob addressed his prayers to God, specifically the God of Abraham and Isaac. (This you may recall is Point #1 in the chapter on Psalms.) Jacob recalled God's promise to do good to him (Point #5). He professed his personal unworthiness before God while also mentioning some of God's character traits (Points #3 and #4). He remembered what God had done for him when he said, "I had only my staff when I crossed this Jordon, but now I have become two camps" (Point #9). He poured out his heart to God, petitioning Him to deliver him from the hand of his brother of whom he was afraid. And Jacob's petition to God is based on God's promises and on His sovereign will (Points # 10, 5, and 7).

This prayer is another classic example of how we should petition God when we are in distress. It should be noted that after praying, Jacob found the faith and courage he needed to face his brother. The late Christian pastor and author Dr. Adrian Rogers once said, "Courage is just fear that has said its prayers."[1] After this prayer was offered, God proved faithful once again by giving Esau a spirit of forgiveness and a heart to receive his brother Jacob.

Hezekiah

In Isaiah 36:7, we read that King Hezekiah was a God-fearing king who tore down altars and high places where the people worshiped other gods. He was also a man of prayer. Two of his prayers are recorded in the book of Isaiah. These prayers were for his city and for himself.

The first of Hezekiah's prayers can be found in Isaiah 37:14-20. He had received a letter informing him that Sennacherib, the king of Assyria planned to invade Jerusalem. Sennacherib challenged Hezekiah, saying if he thought his God could save Israel, his trust was misplaced. When Hezekiah read the letter, he went up to the house of the Lord, spread the letter out before the Lord and prayed. His prayer is recorded in Isaiah 37:16-20.

"Lord Almighty, the God of Israel, enthroned between the cherubim, you alone are the God over all the kingdoms of the earth. You have made heaven and earth. Give ear, Lord, and hear; open your eyes, Lord, and see; listen to all the words Sennacherib has sent to ridicule the living God.

It is true, Lord, that the Assyrian kings have laid waste all these peoples and their lands. They have thrown their gods into the fire and destroyed them, for they were not gods but only wood and stone, fashioned by human hands. Now, Lord our God, deliver us from his hand, so that all the kingdoms of the earth may know that you, Lord, are the only God."

In this prayer, Hezekiah's sole basis for asking for God's help was the fact that God's name was at stake. Hezekiah admitted that he was facing a formidable opponent. Sennacherib had conquered all the nations he had come against thus far. But Hezekiah reminded God and himself that the other nations did not serve a real God who could protect them, like Israel did.

God heard Hezekiah's prayer and sent word back through the prophet Isaiah that the only reason Sennacherib had become great in the first place was because God had determined it would be that way long ago. In Isaiah 37:26-35, God said to Sennacherib, "Have you not heard? Long ago I ordained it. In the days of old I planned it; now I have brought it to pass, that you have turned fortified cities into piles of stone."

God added, "Because you have raged against me ... I will put my hook in your nose ... and I will make you return by the way you came ... I will defend this city and save it, for my sake and for the sake of David, my servant." Then, according to Isaiah 37:36-37, God sent His angel who struck down 185,000 in the camp of the Assyrians. The next day the people found only dead bodies. Sennacherib went home the way he came, just as God said he would.

In the other recorded prayer, Hezekiah prayed on his own behalf when he became sick to the point of death. Isaiah 38:2-3 says, "Hezekiah turned his face to the wall and prayed to the Lord. 'Remember, Lord, how I have walked before you faithfully and with wholehearted devotion and have done what is good in your eyes.' And Hezekiah wept bitterly."

Hezekiah is obviously pouring out his heart to God in this passage. God answered this heartfelt prayer favorably. In Isaiah 38:5, God said,

"I have heard your prayer and seen your tears: I will add fifteen years to your life." After hearing the news that he would live, Hezekiah praised God, in Isaiah 38:17-19, saying, "In your love you have kept me from the pit of destruction … For the grave cannot praise you, death cannot sing your praise … The living, the living—they praise you, as I am doing today."

Hezekiah's prayers reinforce some of the Biblical truths that we have seen before. Once again, we see a prayer warrior petitioning God for God's own namesake, pouring out his heart to God, and giving God praise and thanksgiving for answered prayers.

Solomon

Solomon was King David's son. He ascended to the throne after his father's death. King Solomon was the wisest man who ever lived as well as the richest and grandest king of his day. Two of his prayers are recorded in the Bible.

The first of these appears in two places, 1 Kings 3:5-14 and 2 Chronicles 1:7-12. In this prayer, Solomon requested that God grant him wisdom. God told Solomon to "Ask for whatever you want me to give you." To this Solomon responded:

"You have shown great kindness to your servant, my father David, because he was faithful to you … You have continued this great kindness to him and have given him a son to sit on his throne this very day.

Now, Lord my God, you have made your servant king in place of my father David. But I am only a little child and do not know how to carry out my duties … So give your servant a discerning heart to govern your people and to distinguish between right and wrong."

This prayer reflects much of what we have seen before in the prayers of Solomon's father David. Like David, Solomon approached God from a position of humility. He said, "I am only a little child. I do not know how to carry out my duties." Also like David, Solomon remembered God's character trait of love. He recalled how God had shown this love to his father. Only after this did Solomon make his request to God for the gift of wisdom. Solomon ended his prayer at a point of humility by asking, "For who is able to govern this great people of yours?"

Solomon's response pleased God. This sheds light on the type of prayer that pleases God—a prayer made from a point of humility, or personal unworthiness, in which God is exalted and acknowledged for who He is, what He has done, and what He will do. God's pleasure with Solomon can be seen in 1 Kings 3:10-12, which reads:

"The Lord was pleased that Solomon had asked for this. So God said to him, 'Since you have asked for this and not for long life or wealth for yourself, nor have asked for the death of your enemies but for discernment in administering justice, I will do what you have asked. I give you a wise and discerning heart, so that there will never have been anyone like you, nor will there ever be.'"

God added to this gift of wisdom, which he had given to Solomon. In 1 Kings 3:13-14 God also gave him riches and honor and a conditional promise of a long life, if he would continue to keep God's commandments.

Unfortunately, we know from 1 Kings 11:9 that Solomon did not walk in God's ways all his life. After all God had done for him, Solomon turned away from the Lord and followed after false gods. When he was old, his foreign wives, whom he should never have married, turned his heart after other gods. Sadly, in his old age, Solomon's heart was no longer completely true to the Lord his God.

The second of Solomon's prayers is a long one that can be found in 1 Kings 8:22-53 and 2 Chronicles 6:12-22. This prayer was made at the formal dedication of the Temple. First Kings 8:22-28 says:

"Then Solomon stood before the altar of the Lord in front of the whole assembly of Israel, spread out his hands towards heaven and said: 'Lord, the God of Israel, there is no God like you ... you who keep your covenant of love to your servants who continue wholeheartedly in your way. You have kept your promise to your servant David my father ...

Now, Lord ... keep for your servant David my father the promises you made to him ...

But will God really dwell on earth? ... even the highest heavens cannot contain you. How much less this temple I built! Yet, give attention to your servant's prayer and plea for mercy ... Hear the cry of the prayer that your servant is praying in your presence this day.'"

Solomon's prayer went on for many more verses stipulating specific situations in which the children of Israel might sin and suffer the consequences for their sins. Each time, Solomon requested that when the consequences come, and the people pray to God, for Him to hear their prayers, forgive them, and rescue them from those consequences. Solomon ended his prayer in 1 Kings 8:52-53 with, "May your eyes be open to your servant's plea and to the plea of your people Israel, and may you listen to them whenever they cry out to you. For you singled them out from all the nations of the world to be your own inheritance."

In this prayer, Solomon did not articulate as much personal humility or brokenness as we have seen in other prayers. Rather, he expressed the corporate humility of the people by drawing a contrast between the children of Israel and the mighty God they served. An example of this is in 1 Kings 8:23 when he said, "There is no God like you in heaven above or earth below." He noted his personal humility along with the peoples' when he referred to them and himself as servants. He called himself a servant even though he was the richest king who had ever lived. Solomon also remembered God's promises and His deeds. He petitioned God for continued involvement in the lives of the people to forgive them and help them when they cried out to Him in need.

Jehoshaphat

Jehoshaphat was one of Judah's kings during a time when the nation of Israel was split into the two kingdoms of Israel and Judah. Although his father Asa had been a wicked king, Jehoshaphat was godly. Second Chronicles 17:3-4 (ESV) says, "The Lord was with Jehoshaphat because he walked in the earlier ways of David. He did not seek the Baals but sought God and walked in His commandments."

There was a time when some armies came against Jehoshaphat intending to do battle with his armies. Afraid, Jehoshaphat set his face to seek the Lord. He proclaimed a fast throughout all Judah and had

Judah to assemble and seek help from the Lord. Jehoshaphat's prayer as found in the twentieth chapter of 2 Chronicles reads,

"Lord, God of our ancestors, are you not the God who is in heaven? You rule over all the kingdoms of the nations. Power and might are in your hand, and no one can withstand you. Our God, did you not drive out the inhabitants of this land before your people Israel and give it forever to the descendants of Abraham your friend? They have lived in it and have built in it a sanctuary for your Name, saying, 'If calamity comes upon us, whether the sword of judgment, or plague or famine, we will stand in your presence before this temple that bears your Name and will cry out to you in our distress, you will hear us and save us.'

But now here are men of Ammon, Moab and Mount Seir … coming to drive us out of the possession you gave us as an inheritance. Our God, will you not judge them? For we have no power to face this vast army that is attacking us. We do not know what to do, but our eyes are on you."

This prayer is reminiscent of all of the other prayers we have seen. Are you growing tired of having the same things pointed out over and over? I can assure you, nothing in the Bible is accidental or random. If God shows us something this many times, He did so for a reason. He must know we are slow learners, and like children, we need to have things repeated many times.

At the risk of sounding repetitious, I point out the following: Jehoshaphat, like all the others, directed his prayer to God, praised and exalted God, and recalled God's dealings with previous generations. He also remembered God's promises and reminded God that the glory of His name was at stake. Then, knowing he was on solid ground before God, Jehoshaphat petitioned God to execute judgment on his enemies. He ended his prayer on a note of humility, acknowledging his and his people's weakness and inability to help themselves. This is seen in verse twelve where it said, "For we have no power to face this vast army … We do not know what to do, but our eyes are on you."

By placing their eyes on God, Jehoshaphat was directing the people to look to the Invisible One, similar to what Moses did. In the English Standard Version of the Bible, Hebrews 11:27 says this about Moses, "By faith he left Egypt, not being afraid of the anger of the king, for he endured as seeing him who is invisible." It takes tremendous faith to be able to see the Invisible One.

The answer to Jehoshaphat's prayer can be found in 2 Chronicles 20:15-17. Through the prophet Jahazial, God told Jehoshaphat:

"Do not be afraid or discouraged … For the battle is not yours but God's. Tomorrow march down against them … stand firm and see the deliverance the Lord will give you … Do not be afraid and do not be discouraged. Go down to face them tomorrow and the Lord will be with you."

Jehoshaphat and the people responded to this news with praise and worship. The next few verses of 2 Chronicles say that Jehoshaphat bowed his head with his face to the ground, and all the people fell down before the Lord with him, worshiping the Lord. The Levites stood up to praise the Lord, the God of Israel, with a loud voice. Did you notice the timing of their praise? The people praised and worshiped *before* they saw the actual victory.

Of course, it did come about just as God had said it would. As it turned out, the invading armies ended up fighting each other. The men of Judah were handed a victory by God and they had only to stand their ground just as God had promised.

QUESTIONS FOR REFLECTION

Abraham

What do Abraham's prayers teach us?

What practical lesson do we learn from Abraham about dealing with challenging situations, times when we are discouraged and our faith is tested?

Jacob

What effect did prayer have on Jacob and how does the late Adrian Rogers state this truth?

Solomon

Solomon's prayer for wisdom sheds light on the type of prayer that pleases God. What elements does a prayer that pleases God contain?

Hezekiah

In addition to praying for others, what else does Hezekiah's second prayer show it is all right to pray?

Jehoshaphat

What is particularly interesting about the timing of the people of Judah's praise in regards to Jehoshaphat's prayer?

Chapter 6: Job

The story of Job is one of the most familiar stories in the Bible. The book of Job includes many of Job's prayers, when prayer is defined as any words directed towards God. Before looking at these prayers, however, it would be good to have an overview of Job's situation.

Job 1:1 tells us that Job was blameless and upright, that he feared God and shunned evil. Job was also wealthy, successful, and highly respected. However, Satan successfully petitioned God for permission to test him within certain limits. In Job 1:12, God tells Satan, "Everything he has is in your power, but on the man himself do not lay a finger." God later amended this restriction in Job 2:6, telling Satan that Job too was in Satan's hands to do harm, but he could not take Job's life.

The interaction between God and Satan teaches us some lessons. One is that when someone is facing difficulties in life, it is not necessarily because of sin or wrongdoing on that person's part. Sometimes God simply allows people to undergo a period of testing. Another point we can take away from this interaction is that Satan cannot do anything that God has not allowed. No matter how it may seem, God is always in control of every situation.

In Job 1:13-2:9 Satan takes away Job's wealth, his health, and even his children. Most of the rest of the book of Job are recorded conversations between Job and his wife, Job and his friends, and Job and God. The conversations with God can be viewed as prayers, which are woven throughout the book. In some ways, these prayers are different from the other prayers we have studied. Our study of prayer should look carefully at these passages. Job's words to God begin in Job 7:11-21, with Job saying:

"Therefore, I will not keep silent; I will speak in the anguish of my spirit, I will complain in the bitterness of my soul ... When I think my bed will comfort me and my couch will ease my complaint, even then you frighten me with dreams and terrify me with visions ... Why have you made me your target? Have I become a burden to you? Why do you not pardon my offenses and take away my sins?"

In this initial prayer, we've seen some of these themes before. Job pours out his heart to God. He also recognizes that God is in control and because Job is confused as to why so many calamities have fallen on him, he inquires of God.

One of Job's friends attempts to answer Job's inquiry in Job 8:1. The friends give him poor advice throughout the entire book. Instead of encouraging him, they discourage and accuse him. Occasionally, I find the Bible to be humorous and this verse is one of those places. Job has just cried out to God in pain asking Him, "Why?" Then Job 8:1 says that Bildad the Shuhite replied.

I imagine Bildad thought he was speaking for God but it strikes me as funny that Job asked God a question and Bildad answered.

In Job 9, we see Job expressing his unworthiness. This can be found in words Job directs towards his friends, rather than God. Here are some examples of what Job said to his friends:

"How can mere mortals prove their innocence before God? ... His wisdom is profound, his power is vast … He moves mountains … shakes the earth … speaks to the sun … He alone stretches out the heavens … performs wonders … miracles that cannot be counted … How then can I dispute with him? He is not a mere mortal like me that I might answer him, that we might confront each other in court."

In chapter 10, Job switches from talking to his friends and directs words towards God saying:

"I say to God: Do not declare me guilty, but tell me what charges you have against me … though you know that I am not guilty and that no one can rescue me from of your hand? Your hands shaped me and made me. Will you now turn and destroy me? Remember that you molded me like clay … You gave me life and showed me kindness … If I am guilty—woe to me! Even if I am innocent, I cannot lift up my head, for I am full of shame."

In Job 13:13, Job was beginning to get annoyed with his friends' lack of encouragement and poor counsel. He told them to be quiet and let him speak. Then he continued saying in Job 13:15-16, "Though he slay me, yet I will hope in him; I will surely defend my ways to his face … for no godless person would dare come before him."

In these words, we glimpse the heart of the man Job. He knew that God was all powerful and sovereign and could do whatever He pleased, yet Job also knew that God was his only hope. Job recognized that only the righteous could come into God's presence with their petitions.

Today, we understand Jesus Christ accomplished this righteous status for believers when He died on the cross for our sins. On this side of the cross, we know this truth to mean that we can approach God through Jesus, whose blood has made us righteous. (Yet, even with our position secured through salvation, we'll learn in the next part of this book there are still things that can hinder our prayers.)

What Job was voicing was his awareness that the godless cannot approach the throne of God. But he knew he was a righteous man who loved God and kept His commandments, so he knew he could come before God with his petitions. Job also knew there was nowhere else he could go with his petitions because no one else could answer him or offer help. This is a classic example of what it means to remain persistent in prayer, even when it does not appear that God is answering. Job was ready to accept God's answer to his petition no matter what it was. This attitude is evident when he said, "Though He slay me, yet I will hope in him."

Job continued talking to God in Job 13:17 through all of chapter 14. He asked God to listen to him, a request we saw in the prayers of so many others including Nehemiah, Ezra, David, and Daniel. Job said he knew he would be vindicated. He said this not because he trusted in himself, but because he knew that God was fair and just. This statement exemplifies 1 John 3:21 which says, "If our hearts do not condemn us, we have confidence before God."

Job asked God to show him his sins because he did not know what they were. He had been pursuing personal holiness and was careful not to sin. Remember, in Job 1:1, we learned there was none like him in all the earth. He was a blameless man who turned away from evil. Since he knew he had not been sinning, Job concluded in Job 13:26 that God must be punishing him for the sins of his youth. His concern indicates that as blameless and upright as he was as an adult, even Job apparently had sinned in his youth. What a tremendous encouragement to all parents of teenagers, and to all of us who were once teenagers, too!

In chapter 14, Job expounds on his understanding of God's sovereignty. He says, "A person's days are determined; you have decreed the number of his months and have set limits he cannot exceed." Yet still he reiterates his confidence in God's fairness and love saying, "All the days of my hard service I will wait for my renewal to come … Surely you will count my steps but not keep track of my sin." Job's friends continued to give him poor advice. In chapter sixteen, Job sounded a bit fed up with them, responding in 16:2, "You are miserable comforters, all of you!" Again in Job 17:10 he tells them, "But come on, all of you, try again! I will not find a wise man among you."

Chapter 18 has Job's friends harassing him again. This was ironic considering that their original purpose in coming to Job was to comfort him. Instead, they falsely concluded Job was receiving deserved punishment from God for a sin (or sins) he had committed. This conclusion couldn't be further from the truth. Job had committed no such sin. God was allowing this for His purposes and glory.

Based on their erroneous conclusion, instead of comforting Job, his friends reprimanded him for continuing to claim his innocence. Instead of encouraging him, they discouraged and accused him. We often behave this way, too, don't we? We also assume that if life is going well for a fellow Christian, it is due to God's blessings. Though this may be true, the converse idea that if a Christian brother or sister is facing difficult times, it must be because of God's displeasure with them, is not necessarily true. As finite human beings, we cannot see the whole picture the way God can. With our limited vision, we fall into thinking that God will work according to our ideas of how things should go, when one of God's most wonderful attributes is that He rules and overrules! Christian author Edward T. Welch said it well when he wrote, "God is God. He is not tame or domesticated like we sometimes make him."[1] Like Job's friends, we often try to draw a connection between someone's walk with God and their tangible, physical well being or success in life. However, the book of Job clearly teaches this thinking is faulty.

Job responded to his friends rather boldly in chapter 19 with comments like, "How long will you torment me … shamelessly you attack me … know that God has wronged me … though I call for help, there is no justice. He has blocked my way so I cannot pass; he has shrouded my paths in darkness. He has stripped me of my honor … He tears me down on every side … My relatives have gone away; my closest friends have forgotten me … All my intimate friends detest me; those I love have turned against me."

But then he adds, "I know that my redeemer lives, and that in the end he will stand on the earth … yet in my flesh I will see God."

And there it is again—Job's unshakable faith in a marvelous God. Even as Job accurately claimed that his entire calamity was from God, not because he had sinned, but because God had sovereignly chosen to allow calamity to fall on him, yet he took comfort in the knowledge that his God lives, and he will see Him someday.

In chapter 29:2-3, Job reminisced about the days before his affliction when he said, "How I long for the months gone by, for the days when God watched over me, when his lamp shone on my head and by his light I walked through darkness." Job drew a contrast between his former good days and his current calamity when he said in Job 30:16, "And now my life ebbs away; days of suffering grip me."

Finally, in chapter 38-41, God answers Job.

"Then the Lord spoke to Job out of the storm. He said, 'Who is this that obscures my plans with words without knowledge? Brace yourself like a man; I will question you and you will answer me ... Where were you when I laid the earth's foundation? ... Have you ever given orders to the morning, or shown the dawn its place? ... Have you journeyed to the springs of the sea, or walked in the recesses of the deep? ... Can you bind the chains of Pleiades? Can you loosen Orion's belt? ... Do you send the lightning bolts on their way? ...Will the one who contends with the Almighty correct him?'"

Job's humble and retentive response to God is recorded in chapter 42. He says:

"I know that you can do all things; no purpose of yours can be thwarted ... Surely I spoke of things I did not understand, things too wonderful for me to know ... My ears had heard of you but now my eyes have seen you. Therefore, I despise myself and repent in dust and ashes."

Job's prayers are similar in some ways, while at the same time quite different, from the other prayers in the Old Testament. In most of the other prayers, someone had sinned. This is why the other prayers contained lines that said the people were covered with shame (Daniel), they were obstinate (Moses), and "I am not a man but a worm" (David).

However, in Job's case, he had not sinned and much of his prayer was an effort to make this point to God and to his friends. The overriding lesson we learn from Job's interactions with God is that God is almighty, omnipotent, and sovereign. Even without an overt sin on his part, Job came to see that his defensive attitude was itself sin. This explains why he repented at the end of his prayer. Job came to see, as we all must, that God is a holy and awesome God, and we are but flesh. This point is consistent with other prayers in that the other prayer warriors also approached God from a point of humility. Another similarity is the fact that Job trusted in God's faithfulness and fairness, even when he could not understand what God was doing.

Most Christians know how the book of Job ends. Job 42:10 says, "The Lord restored his fortunes and gave him twice as much as he had before." This is the way we remember the book, which is the way the verse is usually taught in Bible studies. However, we often miss a valuable lesson about prayer in these last few verses. In order to keep from overlooking this important point, let us read carefully the last part of Job. Job 42:7-10:

"After the Lord had said these things to Job, he said to Eliphaz the Temanite, 'I am angry with you and your two friends, because you have not spoken the truth about me, as my servant Job has … My servant Job will pray for you, and I will accept his prayer.' … Eliphaz … Bilbad … and Zophar … did what the Lord told them; and the Lord accepted Job's prayer. After Job had prayed for his friends, the Lord restored his fortunes and gave him twice as much as he had before."

Do you see the lesson? Re-read verse 10. "*After he had prayed for his friends*, the Lord restored his fortunes. Do you see it now? The timing of God's answer to Job's prayers correlates to the time when Job prayed for his friends. My prayer group calls this the "Job method." We tease and say the best way to get our personal prayers answered is to pray for someone else.

One particular day when my prayer group met, and as we shared at the beginning of our time together, I shared a specific answer I had received that week. When I did, one of my friends spoke up excitedly and said that she had been praying specifically about that the past week. Then she told of an answer to one of her prayer requests from the previous meeting and another friend exclaimed that she had been praying that the answer would turn out just that way. Then, that friend shared an answer she had received, causing me to laugh and say, "And I was praying about that! It's the Job method, and it really works!" We all had a good laugh!

Seriously, I don't think it's an accident or coincidence that the timing of God's answer to Job's prayers is connected to the timing of Job's prayer for his friends. Although we do know from other Scriptures that God answers a person's heartfelt prayers for himself, (Hannah), even so, we also know that it pleases God when we pray for others. We see this in the examples of so many Biblical characters such as David, Ezra, Moses, Nehemiah, and many more. As we have seen before, Scripture makes it clear that God looks for a person who will stand in the gap for others as it says in Ezekiel 22:30.

In addition, there are numerous places in the New Testament where we are exhorted to pray for each other. In Job's case, when he finally got his mind off his own problems and was able to show concern for others, God restored his fortunes. Job was a godly man, in whom God took pleasure. He had not sinned and was correct in what he said about himself and about God. Yet, even a man such as this still had some lessons to learn. He learned that God is the same in good times and in bad. He learned that God is in control even when it is difficult to understand what He is doing. He also learned that it is the right thing to do and it pleases God when we pray for others, even others who have mistreated us. "And the Lord blessed the latter days of Job's life more than the former part" (Job 42:12).

QUESTIONS FOR REFLECTION

What does the first chapter of Job teach us about Satan's power to harm us?

What does Job say that helps us know he petitioned God with an open hand, ready to accept God's will regardless of how it affected him?

Throughout most of the book, Job defends himself, claiming to have done no wrong. This claim was true. But towards the end of the book, Job repents. If he had done no wrong, what was Job repenting of?

What often overlooked lesson about prayer can be found in the timing of God's restoration of Job?

New Testament

"When we come to God we are approaching the throne of grace,
not the throne of merit."

Mark Janke
pastor of Franklin Street Church, Louisville, Kentucky

CHAPTER 7: PRAYER IN THE NEW TESTAMENT

The focus of the New Testament with regards to prayer is primarily on teachings about prayer, along with an emphasis on the importance of prayer as demonstrated through the many times people are seen praying. This stands in contrast to the Old Testament where the actual content of certain prayers were recorded. In the Old Testament, we found specific prayer warriors and the words they spoke to God. The New Testament, on the other hand, is rich in teachings about prayer. These teachings come from the apostle Paul, some of the other apostles, and even Jesus Himself. In studying what the New Testament has to say about prayer, we will look at both the teachings as well as the few specific cases of recorded prayer.

Teachings

Perhaps the greatest of the teachings, and possibly the ones that are the most critical for an understanding of prayer are the teachings pertaining to the various roles each member of the Trinity plays in prayer. In a nutshell, the New Testament teaches that prayer is addressed to the Father, through the Son (or in the name of Jesus) and with the help of the Holy Spirit (or in the Spirit). In order to grasp what is meant by this, let's look at each part of the Trinity separately.

The Father

The principle that we should address our prayers to God, the Father, has already been well established through Old Testament examples. It is reinforced in the New Testament as well. Jesus, Himself, taught this, both through instruction and in practice. Some examples of times Jesus prayed to the Father include:

"At that time Jesus said, 'I praise you, Father, Lord of heaven and earth, because you have hidden these things from the wise and learned, and revealed them to little children. Yes, Father, for this is what you were pleased to do'" (Matthew 11:25-26).

"'Father, I thank you that you have heard me. I knew that you always hear me, but I said this for the benefit of the people standing here, that they may believe that you sent me'" (John 11:41-42).

"Now my soul is troubled, and what shall I say? 'Father, save me from this hour'? No, it was for this reason I have come to this hour. Father, glorify your name" (John 12:27-28).

"My Father, if it be possible, may this cup be taken from me. Yet, not as I will but as you will" (Matthew 26:39).

"Father, forgive them, for they do not know what they are doing" (Luke 23:34).

"Father, into your hands I commit my spirit" (Luke 23:46).

In addition, Jesus instructed his disciples to pray to the Father in Matthew 6:9, "This, then, is how you should pray: 'Our Father in heaven, hallowed be your name.'" Jesus also gave teachings that are consistent with the assumption that a person is praying to the Father. For instance in Matthew 6:8, Jesus said, "Your Father knows what you need before you ask him." Again Jesus instructed in Matthew 6:6, "But when you pray, go into your room, close the door and pray to your Father, who is unseen. Then your Father, who sees what is done in secret, will reward you."

The apostle Paul models the practice of praying to the Father as well. Paul says in Ephesians 3:14, "For this reason I kneel before the Father." We see this again in Colossians 1:12 when Paul writes, "and giving joyful thanks to the Father, who has qualified you." And again in Ephesians 5:20 he writes, "always giving thanks to God the Father for everything, in the name of our Lord Jesus Christ."

The Son

We often hear prayers ending with the words, "in Jesus name." As a child, I wondered why prayers ended this way. Now, I understand. The doctrine of the Trinity is a much deeper and more complicated doctrine than I am attempting to cover in this book. But simply put, with regards to Jesus, John 3:16 says He is the only begotten Son of the Father. He is one with the Father according to John 10:30. Yet, we know from John 1:14 that He was also fully man and born of a virgin according to Luke 1:34. We learn from Matthew 27:1—28:20 that He suffered and died on the cross, was buried, and rose again on the third day. John 10:18 lets us know that He willingly laid down His life. When He did this, He made our salvation possible.

Another way of saying this is that we have salvation *through* Christ. Our ability to come to a holy God is *through* His son, Jesus the Christ. Although this is true eternally (after we die), it is also true now while we are alive, when we are praying. That is why the proper way to approach the Father is *through* the Son, or in the name of the Son. This teaching is specified in John 14:6, which says, "Jesus answered, 'I am the way and the truth and the life. No one comes to the Father except through me.'" Paul and the other apostles used the wording "in Jesus name" often in their speeches and writings. Examples of this can be found in some of the books Paul wrote such as Colossians, Thessalonians, and others.

Some specific verses in which we see this wording in the context of prayer are:

"I thank my God through Jesus Christ for all of you" (Romans 1:8).

"Always giving thanks to God the Father for everything, in the name of our Lord Jesus Christ" (Ephesians 5:20).

"And whatever you do, whether in word or deed, do it all in the name of the Lord Jesus" (Colossians 3:17).

"So that in all things God may be praised through Jesus Christ" (1 Peter 4:11).

Perhaps the most descriptive verse of all is 1 Corinthians 8:6 which says, "yet, for us there is but one God, the Father, *from* whom all things come and *for* whom we live; and there is but one Lord, Jesus Christ, *through* whom all things come and *through* whom we live." [emphasis by author]

The Holy Spirit

Second Corinthians 1:22 tells us God's Holy Spirit is freely given to all Christians. He has many functions in our lives. Romans 8:14 says He leads us, John 16:13 says He guides us, Galatians 5:16 says He helps us not sin, Romans 15:16 says He sanctifies us, Ephesians 3:16

says He strengthens us in our walk with Christ, and John 15:26 says He bears witness to us of Jesus Christ.

The Holy Spirit is an active participant in our prayers. One of the best scriptural explanations of the role the Holy Spirit plays in our prayers can be found in Romans 8:26-27. This passage says:

"In the same way, the Spirit helps us in our weakness. We do not know what we ought to pray for, but the Spirit himself intercedes for us with wordless groans. And he who searches our hearts knows the mind of the Spirit, because the Spirit intercedes for God's people in accordance with the will of God."

Wow! It is no wonder that prayer is so powerful. When we pray, we tap into the awesome power of Almighty God. As we pray, His Holy Spirit is right there with us. He knows the perfect will of the Father in a way that we do not. This passage gives me courage to pray anything on my heart because it assures me that even when I do not know God's will in a certain situation, the Holy Spirit who prays with me does. It is comforting to know that where I may pray amiss, the Holy Spirit who is praying with me never does. He adds both direction and strength to my prayer life.

One must remember though, this awesome and powerful resource available to us as we pray is only available *if we actually take the time to pray*! That may seem obvious and yet so many times we think about and even fret over situations, but we do not pray about them. We are too busy, or too preoccupied. How many times have you or I told someone we would pray for them, but then did not? I know I have been guilty of this more times than I like to remember. God convicted me in this area several years ago. Now, if I tell someone I will be praying for him or her, I write it down in my prayer journal so I remember it when I am praying. We have good intentions but we often do not follow through. The Scripture does not say that when we *intend* to pray, the Holy Spirit will pray for us. God's word says that the Holy Spirit helps us *when* we pray. This clearly requires actual prayer on our parts.

Some verses that help us understand better the role of the Holy Spirit in our prayers include:

"And pray in the Spirit on all occasions with all kinds of prayers and requests … be alert and always keep on praying for all the Lord's people" (Ephesians 6:18).

"At that time Jesus, full of joy through the Holy Spirit, said, 'I praise you, Father'" (Luke 10:21).

"The Spirit searches all things, even the deep things of God" (1 Corinthians 2:10).

"Because you are sons, God sent the Spirit of his Son into our hearts'" (Galatians 4:6).

"The Spirit you received does not make you slaves … rather, the Spirit you received brought about your adoption to sonship. And by him we can cry, 'Abba, Father'" (Romans 8:15).

QUESTION FOR REFLECTION

What are the basic roles of the Father, Son, and the Holy Spirit in regards to prayer?

CHAPTER 8: TEACHINGS ON PRAYER

Beyond this most basic teaching concerning the roles of the Trinity, there are numerous other teachings or principles about prayer in the New Testament. Though not an exhaustive list, we'll cover the following principles in this chapter: strengthening our love for others, understanding that prayer is work, increasing the effectiveness of our prayers by understanding what enhances and what interferes with them, the content of our prayers, and the need for persistence in our prayer effort. Finally, we will look at some specific prayers of a few New Testament characters before concluding the book.

Strengthening Our Love for Others

D. A. Carson, in his book *A Call to Spiritual Reformation*, writes, "If we are to improve our praying, we must strengthen our loving. As we grow in disciplined, self-sacrificing love so we will grow in intercessory prayer."[1] This is a true statement but it begs the question—how do we strengthen our love or grow in our love for others?

Growing in love for others is not something we simply will ourselves to do. Regardless of our desire to love others more, growing in love is something we cannot accomplish in the flesh. It is an act of the Holy Spirit. A forced effort to make ourselves become more loving could instead result in a false piety that actually makes us less loving. John Miller in his book *Come Back Barbara* says, "There is no more impenetrable barrier to God's love than the sense of being right."[2] Seeing ourselves as not only right but also loving may perhaps create an even more impenetrable barrier to showing God's love to others.

How do we *truly* become more loving so that we become more fervent in our prayers for others? To begin, we should pray and ask God to make us more loving. If we pray for this with sincere hearts, how do you think God will answer that request? What is the vehicle He often uses to bring about this increased love in us? I think He answers by showing us our own sins. Real love for others can only come about when we see what wretched sinners we ourselves truly are, thereby attaining a greater understanding of the depth of God's love for us. The message of the gospel is that Christ died for us. God forgives us and calls us His children even though we deserve hell.

The seventh chapter of Luke tells the story of a woman who came into a house where Jesus was visiting. Luke 7:38 says, "And she stood behind him at his feet weeping, she began to wet his feet with her tears. Then she wiped them with her hair, kissed them and poured perfume on them." The Pharisee with Jesus responded negatively to this woman's outpouring of love with criticism, saying in Luke 7:39, "If this man were a prophet, he would know who is touching him and what kind of woman she is—that she is a sinner." Jesus replied in verse 47 with, "Therefore, I tell you, her many sins have been forgiven—as her great love has shown. But whoever has been forgiven little loves little."

The love we experience from God directly correlates to the love we are able to extend to others. Am I suggesting we should sin more so we can experience more of God's forgiveness in order to increase our ability to love others? Of course not! I am suggesting instead that we recognize the gravity of the sins we have already committed. Just because our particular sins may not seem as colorful as someone else's, they are still just as potent in their ability to separate us from God. It's obvious from this passage that the Pharisee's sins of being unloving and judgmental towards this woman are just as ugly as whatever sins she may have had. Perhaps the Pharisee's sins were even greater because theirs were sins of the heart and hers were presumably sins of the flesh.

The good news for Christians, saved by Christ's blood, is that no matter how despicable we really are, Christ knows us and He loves us. But in order to strengthen our love for others and therefore our depth of earnestness as we pray for them, we must recognize both that God's love for us is real, and that our sins are horrible. Once we truly acknowledge this, we cannot help but grow in our love for others—the natural by-product of a clear understanding of God's incredible love for us.

Prayer is Work

"Epaphras … a servant of Christ Jesus, sends greetings. He is always wrestling in prayer for you" (Colossians 4:12).

We all desire to have our prayers answered but, sadly, many are not willing to do the work needed to become effective prayer warriors. Prayer is hard work, and like any work, it is at times rewarding but at other times quite grueling. Sometimes we are rejoicing and praising God for answered prayers. Other times we pray and pray and do not seem to see any answers. We have seen this in Scripture many times, haven't we? Several of the Old Testament prayer warriors we studied prayed a long time before they saw answers. Habakkuk, Isaiah, and David even cried out, "How long?" to God. During these times, prayer can seem like hard work.

I have a friend who is a stay-at-home mom. She is a true prayer warrior and I have often heard her say that prayer was her work. This friend is a member of my prayer group. One day she came to prayer group exhausted. She collapsed in her chair and said, "I almost didn't come today. I am catching a cold, I didn't sleep well last night, I don't feel good, and I am tired. But then I thought that if I had job, I would not stay home just because I had a cold and was tired. Well, prayer is my work, so I can't stay home from prayer group just because I am tired, either."[1]

Like work, prayer is time consuming. This is what poses the greatest obstacle to prayer among today's Christians. We live such busy lives that no matter how sincere our intentions, we have trouble finding the time to pray. We should be praying on a regular, daily basis. Remember Daniel? Daniel 6:13 said he prayed three times a day. I remind myself of this fact when I am having trouble finding time in my day to pray even once. No matter how busy I may be, or how pressing the events of my day may seem, I cannot possibly be as busy as Daniel was. He had a nation to run, yet somehow, he managed to find time to pray not just once a day, but three times a day. If he could do that, than surely I can find the time to pray at least once during my day.

Another friend of mine spoke about this problem with me a few years ago. She said "It's no wonder this generation of teenagers is having such a difficult time. People don't pray for them like they used to. I can remember my grandparents sitting at their breakfast table every morning, praying for every member of their family by name. They lifted my name to the Lord every single day. People no longer sit around tables and pray. We are always in such a hurry to get out of the house in the mornings. This is true nationwide and even worldwide.

Thousands and even millions of people used to pray every day by name for others but that no longer happens." [2]

I shared this conversation with my prayer group. Later, one of my friends said, "Remember what you said about praying for your family every day? Well, it has really had an impact on me. Now I do it every day as part of my routine. You know … I brush my teeth, I make my bed, and I pray for each member of my immediate family by name!" [3]

Prayer is like work in another way. Just as work requires the people working keep up their skills in order to continue being effective at their job, prayer requires that the person praying keep up his or her personal walk with God in order to continue praying effectively. This includes paying close attention to personal holiness, Bible study, meditating on God, as well as in fellowship with other believers.

Like work, being an effective prayer warrior demands commitment and effort. Here are some verses, from both the Old Testament and the New Testament, which make this point:

"The eyes of the Lord are on the righteous, and his ears are attentive to their cry" (Psalm 34:15).

"The righteous cry out, and the Lord hears them; he delivers them from all their troubles" (Psalm 34:17).

"Always give yourselves fully to the work of the Lord, because you know that your labor in the Lord is not in vain" (1 Corinthians 15:58).

Elizabeth Elliott is quoted by Chip Ingram in his book *The Invisible War*. Elliott says, "People who ski, I suppose, are people who happen to like skiing, who have the time for skiing … Recently I found that I often treat prayer as though it were a sport like skiing—something you do if you like it, something you do in your spare time … But prayer isn't a sport. It's work. Prayer is no game … prayer is the opposite of leisure. It's something to be engaged in, not indulged in. It's a job you give priority to."[4]

Things that Enhance or Interfere with Our Prayers

This topic could constitute an in-depth study by itself. Volumes of information could be written about this topic, covering everything from Biblical reference books to practical advice. In this book, I will not be making helpful suggestions like journal keeping, scheduling tips, or other practical ways of enhancing one's prayer life. Rather, we will look only at what the Scripture says interferes with, or enhances, our prayers.

Scripture primarily makes two points. Godly living and personal holiness adds strength to our prayers, where as the lack of godly living or personal holiness detracts from our prayers. These also affect our relationship with God as well as our relationships with others.

In regards to how godly living affects our prayers, we are told the following:

"Come near to God and he will come near to you" (James 4:8).

"Be alert and of sober mind so that you may pray" (1 Peter 4:7).

"The Lord is far from the wicked, but he hears the prayer of the righteous" (Proverbs 15:29).

"For the eyes of the Lord range throughout the earth to strengthen those whose hearts are fully committed to him" (2 Chronicles 16:9).

"The prayer of a righteous person is powerful and effective"

(James 5:16).

"Receive from him anything we ask, because we keep his commands and do what pleases him" (1 John 3:22).

Some contrasting verses point out a lack of personal holiness in our lives will interfere with our prayers:

"If I had cherished sin in my heart, the Lord would not have listened" (Psalm 66:18).

"Surely the arm of the Lord is not too short to save, nor his ear too dull to hear. But your iniquities have separated you from your God; your sins have hidden his face from you, so that he will not hear" (Isaiah 59:1-2).

When discussing sin and righteousness we must remember that we are all sinners and our righteousness is through Jesus' blood, alone. Therefore, anyone may offer up prayers to God at any time if he has first confessed his sins and accepted Jesus' sacrifice for those sins. This decision to accept Jesus as the One who saves a person from his sins happens only once. Nonetheless, it is still important to confess our sins on a regular basis in our prayers to remove any block or hindrance to our prayers.

First John 1:9 tells us that God is faithful and just to forgive our sins every time we ask. If we are serious about repentance, we will turn away from our sins and not continue in a pattern of sinning. To fail to do this and to continue to actively sin in an area of our lives will interfere with our prayers as well as our testimony. On the other hand, our prayers will be strengthened if we, with God's help, embrace godliness and turn away from sin.

How we treat others also affects our prayers. Scriptures that speak about this include:

"To share your food with the hungry and to provide the poor wanderer with shelter—when you see the naked, to clothe them ... then you will call, and the Lord will answer; you will cry for help, and He will say: Here am I" (Isaiah 58:7-9).

"Husbands, in the same way be considerate as you live with your wives, and treat them with respect as the weaker partner ... so that nothing will hinder your prayers" (1 Peter 3:7).

"Religion that God our Father accepts as pure and faultless is this: to look after orphans and widows in their distress and to keep oneself from being polluted by the world" (James 1:27).

With regards to all of these areas (our relationships to God, others, and the need for confession of our sins) our roles as intercessors can be summed up in the following verses. "Every high priest is selected from among the people and is appointed to represent the people in matters related to God, to offer gifts and sacrifices for sins. He is able to deal gently with those who are ignorant and are going astray, since he himself is subject to weakness. This is why he has to offer sacrifices for his sins, as well as for the sins of the people" (Hebrews 5:1-3).

Of course, we are intercessors not priests. Priests, as laid out in the Old Testament, no longer exist. This is because the Scripture tells us in Hebrews 5:5-6 that now Jesus Christ is our high priest. Even so, one of the functions of an Old Testament priest was to intercede before God for the people. As we intercede for others in prayer, we should remember the message of this verse so that we too can deal gently with others knowing that we ourselves are beset with weaknesses, too. We should pray for the forgiveness of our own sins so that our prayers for others will be heard by God.

Fasting and Faith

In addition to what we have examined so far, there are a few other teachings about prayer. Two I consider particularly pertinent include the teachings regarding the impact of fasting and faith on our prayer lives.

Fasting

Fasting is a practice found throughout Scripture. It is almost always linked to prayer, often in the context of seeking God accompanied by petitions for mercy, forgiveness, or wellbeing. Conversely, prayer is not always linked to fasting. Just before Jesus ate, He prayed asking God to bless the food. The majority of prayers found throughout Scripture are *not* prayed in the context of fasting. A person can pray without fasting but he should probably not observe a fast without also taking the time to pray while he fasts.

Fasting appears to be a practice that pleases God and adds strength to our prayers, but is not mandatory. Let's look at people in the Bible who fasted, taking note of when, why, and how they practiced it.

Corporate fasting—fasting practiced by a group of people—is found often in the Scriptures. Sometimes, like we find in Zechariah 7:3, this type of fasting is observed on a regular basis. Other times, like in 2 Chronicles 20:3, a fast is declared or proclaimed as a one-time situation. Ezra declared this kind of fast in Ezra 8:21-23.

Many Old Testament characters declared corporate fasts, including Nehemiah, Esther, and King Jehoiakim. Joel recommends corporate fasting in Joel 1:14 and 2:15, and the people of Nineveh practiced corporate prayer in Jonah 3:5 when they were seeking God's forgiveness.

In addition to corporate fasting, personal fasts are also recorded in the Scripture. David fasted many times. We see an instance of this in Psalm 109:24 when he wrote, "My knees give way from fasting; my body is thin and gaunt."

Daniel also fasted. In Daniel 9:3 he says, "So I turned to the Lord God and pleaded with him in prayer and petition, in fasting and sackcloth and ashes."

God, Himself, is recorded as calling for His people to fast on one occasion. This, presumably, was calling for both corporate and personal fasts, and can be found in Joel 2:12. "'Even now,' declares the Lord, 'return to me with all your heart, with fasting and weeping, and mourning.'"

The practice of fasting shows up in the New Testament as well. In Matthew 4:2, Jesus fasted for forty days and forty nights prior to His temptation. The disciples also fasted. They did not fast while Jesus was with them according to Matthew 9:15. However, they did fast later, according to Acts 14:23, after Jesus was no longer with them.

In the New Testament, we find Anna, who seemed to have done nothing but pray and fast. The Bible tells us little about Anna. In Luke 2, we learn she was a prophetess, the daughter of Phanuel, of the tribe of Asher, and she was old. She had been married as a young woman for seven years before she was widowed. She never remarried and was either 84 yrs old or had been widowed for 84 years—the Scriptures are a bit ambiguous on this point but either way, she was quite old. We also know that she stayed in the temple worshiping with fasting and prayer night and day.

Anna was not a queen like Esther or the grandmother of a king like Ruth. She was not the matriarch of a great nation like Sarah. She was not the mother of a great and godly man like Eunice. It is unlikely that Anna was a mother at all. She was not a warrior like Deborah, or a businesswoman like Lydia. She did not sew clothes for the poor like Dorcas. She never held benefits for any causes, visited shut-ins, baked casseroles for church potlucks, or volunteered for mission trips. The list of things Anna did not do could go on and on. She may actually seem rather insignificant and one may wonder why God included her, by name, in His word. What did she have and what did she do that was of any value?

She had a faith in her God, whom she loved so much that she wanted to dwell in His house. She prayed, fasted, and worshiped all the time, day and night. We do not even have a record of what she prayed for as we do for Hannah. Yet, her faithful acts of continual prayer and fasting were noteworthy to the Lord; He recorded it for all mankind to know. God gave her the blessing of seeing the Christ Child as well, whom she recognized as the Messiah when many others did not.

Even though we have no way of knowing what Anna prayed for so diligently, I can't help but wonder if some of her prayers may have been for the coming of the promised Messiah. I surmise this based on several things: she was a prophetess, she recognized the Christ Child when she saw Him, giving thanks to God immediately. God is faithful, and does answer our prayers. So if perhaps she had been praying for the coming of the Messiah, God was faithful in letting her see the answer to her prayers—and a prayer of that magnitude just might require the work of a full time prayer warrior night and day for eighty four years!

In summary, fasting is a practice that we might want to consider incorporating into our prayer lives, if we are serious about prayer. It is certainly taught in the Scripture. Fasting would enhance our prayers and be a blessing to us. Nevertheless, it is not required. Fasting does not make us godly. Scripture records a few occasions where ungodly people fasted. In 1 Kings 21:9, the wicked Queen Jezebel orders some of her people to fast just prior to having an innocent man killed. The Pharisees also fasted according to Matthew 9:14.

To keep fasting in perspective, God gives us Isaiah 58:4-9 and Matthew 6:16-17:

"Your fasting ends in quarreling and strife ... You cannot fast as you do today and expect your voice to be heard on high ... Is not this the kind of fasting I have chosen: to loose the chains of injustice ... to set the oppressed free ... Is it not to share your food with the hungry and to provide the poor wanderer with shelter ... Then you will call, and the Lord will answer" (Isaiah 58:4-9).

"When you fast, do not look somber as the hypocrites do, for they disfigure their faces to show others they are fasting. Truly, I say to you, they have received their reward in full. But when you fast, put oil on your head and wash your face, so that it will not be obvious to others that you are fasting, but only to your Father who is unseen; and your Father who sees what is done in secret will reward you" (Matthew 6:16-18).

Faith

"And without faith it is impossible to please God, because anyone who comes to him must believe that he exists and that he rewards those who earnestly seek him" (Hebrews 11:6).

The nature of the faith we are to have when we pray is often a point of confusion for many Christians. Some believe and even teach that if we only have enough faith when we pray (in other words, if we believe hard enough) then whatever we want to happen *will* happen. I think this confusion is at least in part due to passages like Mark 11:24 where it says, "Therefore I tell you, whatever you ask for in prayer, believe that you have received it, and it will be yours." John 14:13 says, "And I will do whatever you ask in my name."

It is true that these words were spoken by Jesus, and we know that He only and always spoke truth. Yet, when we look at these verses in the context of the whole of Scripture, I don't think Jesus meant by these words that we could tell God what to do, or get God to work according to our agenda. Jesus also said in Matthew 26:39, "Yet, not as I will, but as you will." Jesus uttered these words in the Garden of Gethsemane just before facing the ordeal of the cross. In submitting to the cross, He modeled the act of submitting His will to the Father's.

The truths about faith Jesus spoke in Mark 11:24 and John 14:13 carry with them an unspoken supposition. If we are praying with that level of faith then we are walking closely enough to our Lord to ask things in line with His will, so that the will of God still reigns supreme rather than our will.

In the John 14:13 verse, it should be noted that Jesus stipulated that you must ask in His name. It is possible that asking in Christ's name means that we are asking according to His will. In other words, Christ's name is not a toy or magic word we can use to go about commanding things to happen the way we want them to. Rather, it symbolizes whose service we are in when we pray. We are servants of the King acting on *His* behalf as an agent for bringing about change according to *His* plan.

I had a Christian friend many years ago who died of cancer. When she was in the hospital, as her health was failing, a misguided church group began visiting her. They told her that if she and her husband had enough faith, she would be healed of her cancer. My friend and her husband were both believers. They knew God was real and He *could* heal her if He chose to. In their strong desire for her to be cured of her cancer, they left their church and joined the new church.

What followed was sad to watch. My friend denied reality while claiming healing even as her health failed. She robbed herself of the opportunity to prepare both herself and her loved ones for her impending death. They were denied the opportunity to say their goodbyes.

When she was in the hospital dying, she would sometimes ask for pain medication only to be encouraged by her well-meaning husband not to take any meds, because to him and their new church, admission of pain was an indication that her faith was weak. My friend endured unnecessary and grueling pain. She died just the same. Her husband learned the hard way that we cannot manipulate God. Psalm 115:3 says, "Our God is in heaven; he does whatever pleases him."

After her death, the new church group abandoned her family, believing that her death was a result of her and her family's lack of faith. They went on to prey on their next hurting and dying victim to whom they would offer false hope in the name of faith.

The extra pain and crises of faith a belief like this brings is not the most appalling consequence of this misinterpretation of the role faith plays in prayers. Most appalling is that this belief causes us to take the glory for answered prayers for ourselves rather than giving it to God. When our prayers are answered the way we had hoped, instead of others proclaiming, "Look what God has done!" they will exclaim, "Look at what great faith you have!" This belief perpetuates the errant idea that God has no choice but to grant our petitions if our faith is strong enough. It implies that either our faith can trump God's will, or that God has no will until we show Him through our faith what His will is to be. It strongly implies that we are stronger and more powerful than God, in that we can control what God does.

Faith is important in our prayers. But the real question is the focus of that faith. When we pray, are we focused on the request or the God who answers? The God we must put our faith in is a God who can do anything. He can heal the sick, change the weather, meet our needs, forgive sins, change hearts, and uproot satanic strongholds. He is all knowing, all present, and all powerful. Yes, we can ask Him anything. More often than not we ask too little of Him instead of too much.

With our petitions, we need always to be aware God is in control, not us. Things may happen in our lives or in the lives of others that we do not understand, or like. When it does, God has not lost control nor is He less than able. When we cannot understand the events in our lives, we're reminded we cannot see the whole picture.

This point was impressed upon me a few years ago. At the time, I was reading 1 Samuel 15 in my daily devotions. You may remember this passage from our earlier study. When Samuel told Saul that God was going to take the kingdom from him, he knew this was God's will. Yet, the Scripture tells us he grieved over this.

I am not trying to pick on Samuel, and as far as I can tell this is the only time he even came close to displaying wrongful behavior, but from this passage we can conclude that at least to some degree Samuel's heart may have not been in full agreement with God's will. He grieved the loss of Saul as king.

But Samuel did not know David. He did not live to see David as king. We have the story of David and his reign recorded in the Bible so we are able to know what Samuel did not know. We know that David was a man after God's own heart, as stated in Acts 13:22. We know from Matthew 1:17 that Jesus, God's redemption for the world, came through the line of David. We are able to benefit from David's precious writings as recorded in the Psalms. We see the whole story. Samuel did not have our vantage point. All Samuel saw was the loss of Saul, so Samuel grieved.

As this truth about Samuel dawned on me, I prayed and asked God to keep me from ever grieving any turn of events in my life. I asked Him to help me accept His will, always. I determined in my heart to have enough faith to greet whatever came into my life with rejoicing. As so often happens, a few weeks later, I had a seemingly devastating turn of events in my life. Not only did I not receive the new set of circumstances with rejoicing as I had said I would, I confess I was sorely tempted to grieve!

At first, I felt like a complete failure for my inability to rejoice. But as I began to pick up the pieces of this new situation, it occurred to me that as always, God was one step ahead. I was encouraged to realize God had prepared me for what was coming by having me read this story about Samuel. It was helpful to remember that I was not seeing the whole picture. This is what faith is all about when we pray— knowing that God sees what we cannot. "Now faith is the assurance of things hoped for, the conviction of things not seen" (Hebrews 11:1 ESV).

An example of a prayer offered in faith can be found in Philippians 1:19. Paul writes, "For I know that through your prayers and God's provision of the Spirit of Jesus Christ, what has happened to me will turn out for my deliverance." However, in the next few verses he speaks at length about the possibility of dying. Even as Paul was asking for prayers of deliverance, he recognized God might choose to take his life. Paul knew even in the event of his death, God's will would have been fulfilled and his prayers would have been answered. He knew that death too would have been deliverance. He says in verse 21, "For to me, to live is Christ and to die is gain."

I'll end this section on faith with one of my favorite stories of a prayer prayed in faith. When my parents were serving in Nigeria as missionaries, there was a chicken pox epidemic in their village. Many were sick and some had died.

As a physician, my father knew that the chicken pox germs were dispersed in the air whenever someone coughed or sneezed. In addition, the natives were burning their fields, something they did once a year. My father thought the sooty air was further carrying the germs to the people. The germs would float around until they were breathed in by someone, infecting that person. My dad knew that a heavy rain would wash the germ droplets out of the air, ending, or at least dramatically reducing, the rate of infections. This was foremost on his mind one Wednesday evening as he attended a prayer service, because he had just come from the bed of a seven year old child who died from chicken pox and the pneumonia that often accompanies it.

At this service, my father voiced a prayer asking God to send a heavy rain. My father was so focused on the need for rain that it did not even occur to him how unrealistic his request was, since it was the middle of the dry season.

Tropical countries like the one my parents served have only two seasons, rainy and dry. During the rainy season, it rains at least once a day for six months. But during the dry season, it doesn't rain at all for six months. My father's prayer was offered in the middle of the dry season! Many of the other missionaries teased him about it after the prayer meeting ended. Well, guess what? It did indeed rain! And it did not just rain, it stormed! A rare rain storm came up that was so strong it blew off large sections of the hospital's tin roof. The other missionaries did not tease my father any more. They stood in awe of an amazing God![1]

QUESTIONS FOR REFLECTION

Strengthening your Love

Renowned author D. A. Carson writes, "If we are to improve our prayers, we must strengthen our loving." According to Luke 7, how do we accomplish this goal?

Love for others is a natural by-product of what?

How does Jesus explain this truth in Luke 7:47?

Prayer is Work

List three ways in which prayer is like work.

Finish this quote by Elizabeth Elliott:

"Prayer is no game _____ __ ___ _____ __ _____.

It is something to be engaged in, not _____ __."

Things that Enhance or Interfere with Prayer

The Scriptures primarily make two points regarding what enhances and what detracts from our prayers. What are these two points?

Break it down a bit more: Personal holiness (our personal walk with God through reading and observing His word, spending time with Him in prayer and worship, etc.), or the lack thereof, reflects what? Godly living or the lack thereof reflects what?

Fasting and Prayer

Is fasting mandatory?

Why then do we fast?

What should be the focus of our faith when we pray?

If we truly have faith when we pray, does that mean we will always get what we ask for in prayer?

CHAPTER 9: MORE TEACHINGS ON PRAYER

Praise and Thanksgiving

"Enter his gates with thanksgiving and his courts with praise; give thanks to him and praise his name" (Psalm 100:4).

As we studied the Old Testament, the importance of including praise and thanksgiving in our prayers was clearly established. Its importance is reiterated in the New Testament as well. Jesus modeled it in Matthew 11:25. The disciples broke into spontaneous praise to God for the miracles they witnessed in Luke 19:37. A lame beggar leapt in praise after being healed by Peter in Acts 3:9. These examples of praise came in response to seeing God's miracles and experiencing His healing power. But what about praise when we are hurting and pouring our hearts out to God? Is it appropriate then?

Hopefully, after reading the Old Testament part of this book, you know the answer to that question. Do you remember what David said about praise in the Psalms? David made it clear that praise is a choice and an important part of communing with God regardless of circumstances. He said in Psalm 69:30-31, "I will praise God's name … this will please the Lord" after having just said in the preceding verse that he was afflicted and in pain.

Job made this point as well. In Job 2:10, he said, "Shall we accept good from God and not trouble?"

When I was twenty years old, I received the news that one of my best friends from high school had been murdered. She was found face down in a creek having been shot twice in the back of her head. Her college boyfriend, who was with her at the time, was also murdered. He was shot in the back of his head as well, then his body along with his truck were doused with gasoline and set on fire. This double murder remains unsolved to this day.

My friend and I had been cheerleaders together. Our senior year she was the captain of our squad and I was her co-captain. Our football team won the state championship that year. I knew her well and I knew that she was a believer. We roomed together at cheerleading camp both our junior and senior years. She initiated a devotional time each night of camp, both years. I had brought my Bible, but to be honest, I likely would have collapsed in my bed and fallen asleep after the long days of competitions without even opening it, had she not pulled out her Bible and suggested that we take turns sharing our favorite verses with each other. After our team won the state football championship, I watched her as she bravely gave thanks to God in a speech she delivered before our entire, secular, high school. Our city was in shock at the news of her murder.

There was standing room only at her funeral for the many who had not come early enough to get a seat. I sat in a pew, in a room of stunned and grief stricken people listening as my friend's youth pastor attempted to comfort us with God's perspective on this awful situation. Is giving praise and thanksgiving to God appropriate in a situation like this? How can someone possibly be expected to praise God in all circumstances when these are the circumstances?

I don't remember this youth pastor's name or much of what he said at my friend's funeral but I do remember some. At one point, he turned to my friend's grieving parents and said, "God knows what you are going through because God too had a child who died a brutal death at the hands of wicked men." Then he said to the whole congregation, "God has taken the worst thing man can do and redeemed it for Himself. She is with Him now and we can thank Him for that."[1] He followed with a prayer of thanksgiving. So yes, giving praise and thanksgiving *is* a choice we make and it *can* be offered in all circumstances.

"Let us continually offer to God a sacrifice of praise—the fruit of the lips that openly profess his name" (Hebrews 13:15).

"Do not be anxious about anything, but in every situation, by prayer and petition, with thanksgiving, present your requests to God" (Philippians 4:6).

The Content of our Prayers

We covered this subject extensively in an earlier section of this book. In the section about David and the Psalms, we found that our prayers should be directed to the Father. They should contain confessions of our sins, along with praise and thanksgiving. We can also bring our petitions and requests to God as we pour our hearts out to Him. These petitions are often based on God's character, His ability to answer, His promises, His will, and for His glory. The New Testament adds the additional insight that our prayers are made through Jesus Christ with the help of the Holy Spirit.

A few other points are taught or re-emphasized in the New Testament as well. Acts 4:24-30 reminds us by the disciples' example of the importance of quoting Scripture back to God in our prayers. These passages say:

"When they heard this, they raised their voices together in prayer to God. 'Sovereign Lord,' they said, 'you made the heavens and earth and the sea, and everything in them. You spoke by the Holy Spirit through the mouth of your servant, our father David ... The kings of the earth rise up and the rulers band together ... against the Lord and against his anointed one ... Now Lord ... Stretch out your hand to heal.'"

Some versions of the Scripture use the word supplication when they speak of prayer. For instance, in the English Standard Version as well as some others, we are told to pray with supplication in Ephesians 6:18. The ESV says, "Praying at all times in the Spirit, with all prayer and supplication." Again, in Philippians 4:6, the ESV and some others use the word supplication when it says, "do not be anxious about anything, but in everything by prayer and supplication with thanksgiving let your requests be mad known to God."

What exactly is supplication? The dictionary says to supplicate is "to make a humble entreaty; to ask earnestly and humbly." The dictionary also lists as synonyms for supplicate the words, "beseech, implore, beg, and plead."[1] Supplication, therefore, presents a picture of a person humbly but earnestly pouring his heart out to God. I am again reminded of Hannah in her desperate prayer for a child.

Another point made in the Philippians 4:6 passage worth noting is the directive to be anxious for nothing. This directive is linked immediately with another, that of praying about everything. Of course, there's a correlation between the two. If we are praying, then regardless of our situation, we can keep from being anxious, knowing that Psalm

65:2 is true—God is a God who hears prayer. A quote by the late pastor Adrian Rogers that has been cited once already in this book bears repeating here. Dr. Rogers said, "Courage is just fear that has said its prayers."[2]

The New Testament, like the Old Testament, reminds us to pray not just for ourselves but also for others. The New Testament provides numerous examples of Christians praying for others. In his writings, Paul referenced those who were praying for him many times. Paul also mentioned that he was praying for others. When Peter was in prison, in the twelfth chapter of Acts, his escape was a direct result of the prayers of others. I am particularly fond of this passage because after Peter escaped, he ran to the home where the prayer meeting was being held. When he arrived though, the people who were praying for his escape did not believe that it had really happened. Acts 12:12-16 says:

"He went to the house of Mary the mother of John … where many people had gathered and were praying. Peter knocked at the outer entrance, and a servant named Rhoda came to answer the door. When she recognized Peter's voice, she was so overjoyed she ran back without opening it and exclaimed, 'Peter is at the door!'

'You're out of your mind,' they told her. When she kept insisting that it was so, they said, 'It must be his angel.'

But Peter kept on knocking, and when they opened the door and saw him, they were astonished."

Isn't this so like us? Aren't we also guilty of praying about something, even fervently praying about it, yet being amazed and in disbelief when God answers it?

The New Testament teaches us not only that we should pray for others who are our friends and co-workers in the Lord's service, it also teaches that we should pray for our enemies. Luke 6:27-28 says, "Love your enemies, do good to those who hate you, bless those who curse you, pray for those who mistreat you." Jesus modeled this in Luke 23:34 when He prayed for the people who were crucifying Him. As He was dying, He said, "Father, forgive them."

One of my personal favorite prayers for others is derived from the eighth and ninth chapters of Luke, where we are told of a man who was demon possessed. For a long time, this man had worn no clothes and lived among the tombs instead of in a house. The demon seized the man many times, causing him to break the bands that restrained him and driving him out to the desert.

We find another story of a demon possessed man in Luke 9. The man in this story would scream and maul himself. In both stories, Jesus cast out the demons in these men. Luke 8:35 says that after the first man had his demons cast out, "and the people went out to see what had happened … they found the man … sitting at the Jesus' feet, dressed and in his right mind." What a marvelous condition to find a person or to be in ourselves—clothed, in our right mind, and sitting at the feet of Jesus.

I work in a school setting. All too often, I see teenagers who remind me of these demon possessed men. It is not my intention to get into a discussion of demon possession in this book. Although I do believe demon possession exists today, I do not believe a Christian can be *possessed*. However, Christians (and all people) can be *oppressed* by demons. I think this happens more than we realize.

Our fallen world is full of oppression. I see teenagers all the time who, although likely not possessed, seem to resemble the demon possessed men in these verses. Like the demon-possessed men who mauled themselves, these teenagers self-mutilate through cutting or burning. The demon possessed men wore no clothes, and many teenagers wear little and revealing clothes. The men broke their restraints and spent time in the desert. Our teenage culture today is completely unrestrained. Many are in their own spiritually dry deserts of depression and loneliness. Also, like the demon possessed men who lived among the tombs, our teen culture glorifies death in so many ways. Many contemplate and even attempt suicide.

When I see students in my classes who are struggling in some of these areas, I pray for them. I ask God to heal them, to bring them once again to a place where they are in their right mind (one that is anchored in a Christian worldview), clothed (discreet and appropriate in their dress and behavior), and sitting at the feet of Jesus (living close to Him and learning from Him). What an awesome prayer for us all!

The Need for Persistence in our Prayers

What are we to do or think when it seems like our prayers are not being answered? It is possible that we are praying amiss, but it is equally possible that we just need to continue praying. Sometimes God seems to answer our prayers almost immediately but other times He doesn't seem to answer for years. Elijah only prayed one time for God to send fire from heaven and God answered him immediately. Yet, Elijah had to pray seven times, searching earnestly each time before God sent the promised rain. Perhaps Elijah was tempted to quit praying for the rain after one time. Surely, he was tempted to quit after six times! But he did not stop until he knew his prayers were being answered.

The New Testament reiterates the importance of persistence in our prayers. First Thessalonians 5:17 tells us to pray continually. Acts 1:14 says, "They all joined together constantly in prayer." Romans 12:12 exhorts us to be "joyful in hope, patient in affliction, faithful in prayer."

Anna is a great example of someone who persevered in prayer. Though we don't know what she prayed for, we do know that she prayed and fasted for many, many years.

The best passages that emphasize the importance of persistence can be found in Luke 11:5-9 and Luke 18:1-8. These say:

"Suppose one of you has a friend and goes to him at midnight, and says to him, 'Friend, lend me three loaves of bread, because a friend of mine on a journey has come to me, and I don't have anything to offer him.' Then he will answer from inside and say, 'Don't bother me! The door is already locked, and my children and I have gone to bed. I can't get up and give you anything.' I tell you even though he won't get up and get him anything … yet because of his friend's persistence, he will get up and give him as much as he needs. So I say to you, keep asking and it will be given to you. Keep searching and you will find. Keep knocking and the door will be opened to you" (Luke 11:2-9 HCSB).

In Luke 18:1-8 we read,

"Then Jesus told his disciples a parable to show them that they should always pray and not give up. He said: 'In a certain town there was a judge who neither feared God nor cared what people thought. And there was a widow in that town who kept coming to him with the plea, 'Grant me justice against my adversary.' For some time he refused. But finally he said to himself, 'Even though I don't fear God or care what people think, yet because this widow keeps bothering me, I will see that she gets justice' ... And the Lord said, "Listen to what the unjust judge says. And will not God bring about justice for his chosen ones, who cry to him day and night? ... I tell you, he will see that they get justice, and quickly."

This last verse seems to contradict the argument that we should remain persistent. This verse seems to say that God will answer speedily. A passage in Daniel may shed some light on this. In Daniel 9 we read where Daniel began praying to God about a particular issue. Daniel 9:3 says, "So I turned to the Lord God and pleaded with him by prayer and petition, in fasting and in sackcloth and ashes."

Yet we do not find the answer to his prayer until nearly two chapters later. In Daniel 10:10-20, we find Daniel having an encounter with what an angel. This is an extremely interesting passage where we get a glimpse into the nature of spiritual warfare. In Daniel 10:12-13 the angel says, "Do not be afraid, Daniel. Since the first day that you set your mind to gain understanding and to humble yourself before your God, your words were heard, and I have come in response to them. But the prince of the Persian kingdom resisted me twenty-one days. Then Michael, one of the chief princes, came to help me."

Later, in Daniel 10:20-21, after the angel gave Daniel the message he was sent to give, the angel said, "Soon I will return to fight against the prince of Persia, and when I go, the prince of Greece will come ... (No one supports me against them except Michael, your prince ...)"

Wow! What a fascinating passage! The picture as I see it is one of extreme warfare in the spiritual realm. It implies that nations have angelic or demonic spirits associated with them. This passage also seems to indicate that Michael, the archangel, is the angelic spirit associated with the Jewish people.

The exact role of these beings could constitute another book. For the purposes of this book, we will suffice with an overview. We know from Hebrews 1:14 that angels are ministering spirits. They minister to God's people in many ways. They bring warnings and announcements from God. We see this angelic function throughout Scripture. The angel who came in response to Daniel is one such example. In the New Testament, we see another example in Acts 10:3 when an angel appeared to Cornelius. They provide protection to believers, according to Psalm 91:11; they provide deliverance like in Acts 12:7 when an angel delivered Peter from prison; and they care for believers at the moment of death according to Luke 16:22. In addition, angels are seen numerous times in the book of Revelation as God's servants who execute His judgments that He decrees. But exactly how they affect nations, I do not know.

This brief discussion of angels may be interesting but the real point is that according to the passage in Daniel, God did "judge speedily" as the Luke 18:8 passage says. The angel was dispatched as soon as Daniel began praying. However, he was held up due to spiritual warfare. This shows us yet another possible reason our prayers are not always answered immediately. The reality of spiritual warfare should motivate us even more to remain persistent in our prayers because prayer is a strong weapon for fighting spiritual battles.

As we remain persistent in prayer, we need to also remember that God's timing is not necessarily our timing. I tease and say that God has me on a two and a half year schedule. If someone has a prayer request, and asks me to pray for it, I will pray regularly, and in two and a half years, it will be answered. I don't mean to be irreverent with my joking.

Praying about a situation over time and watching eagerly and expectantly for it even (and especially) if the answer doesn't come right away still offers merit. Praying is like exercising to build up the muscles in your body. A person doesn't lift weights and expect to see a difference the next day. However, if a person is persistent in his efforts, he will see a difference over time. Indeed, God's timing is not always our timing, but it is always perfect.

Why does God choose to work this way? I have no answers, but I have some observations. It seems to be the nature of prayer to grow stronger with repetition. Not only does the person praying grow stronger in his prayers, but also the answers to the prayers become more and more evident with time and additional prayers. If people are persistent in their prayers, they can expect to see a difference over time. Prayer seems to have a cumulative effect. Perhaps these truths are for our benefit, so we will grow stronger in our faith and determination with persistence. Maybe God never intended prayer to work like a vending machine, we pray and the answer just pops out. Maybe instead, prayer is work to be done daily.

QUESTIONS FOR REFLECTION

Praise and Thanksgiving

Should praise and thanksgiving be offered to God even in sad or difficult circumstances?

The Content of our Prayers

As a means of review, list (again) some of the elements that should be included in our prayers. (This is a review of the David/Psalms chapter from the Old Testament section of this book.)

What does the word supplication mean?

What are synonyms for supplication?

In the last part of this section, I told the story of the demon possessed man. What was his condition after the demon had been cast out of him? (Hint: It is a condition that we would all do well to be in and one that I often recite in my prayers as a condition I ask God to put me and others in.)

The Need for Persistence in our Prayers

List some possible reasons why our prayers are not always answered immediately.

CHAPTER 10: JESUS

In addition to these teachings, it is helpful to look at some of the prayer warriors in the New Testament and give attention to their prayer life. The New Testament characters we will look at include Paul, and some of the disciples and early Christians. First, however, it is important to see how Jesus prayed.

Jesus is so much more than a prayer warrior! Focusing on only that one aspect of Him seems almost irreverent. Jesus is the Christ, the Son of the living God. John 1 tells us that He is the Word become flesh. He was in the beginning with God. All things came into being by Him and apart from Him nothing came into being that now exists. In Him was life and the life was the light of the men. He is Emmanuel, God with us according to Matthew 1:23. He is the fulfillment of Isaiah 9:6-7— a child born for us, a Son given to us, a wonderful counselor, mighty God, eternal Father, the Prince of Peace. The government rests on His shoulders and there is no end to the increase of His government or of His peace. John 1:29 says He is the Lamb of God who takes away the sins of the world. Isaiah 53:6 explains that He was pierced through for our transgressions, crushed for our sins, and by His scourging we are healed. Matthew 28:6 tells us the good news—that He rose from the dead just as He said He would. And 1 Timothy 6:15 adds that He reigns forever as King of kings and Lord of Lords.

We are allowed a glimpse of Christ's glory in Revelation 1:13-16 where it says:

"… someone like a son of man, dressed in a robe reaching down to his feet and with a golden sash around his chest. The hair on his head was white like wool, as white as snow, and his eyes were like blazing fire. His feet were like bronze glowing in a furnace, and His voice was like the sound of rushing waters. In his right hand he held seven stars, and coming out of his mouth was a sharp, double-edged sword. His face was like the sun shining in all its brilliance."

[Note: The double-edged sword is a reference to the word of God. Hebrews 4:12 tells us that the word of God is quick and powerful and sharper than a two edged sword. Thus, what comes out of Christ's mouth is God's word.]

In light of all of this, it seems almost inappropriate to study only Jesus' prayers, but for the purpose of this book, that is precisely what we will do.

When we think of Jesus' prayers, the first one that usually comes to mind is what is often referred to as the Lord's Prayer. It can be found in Matthew 6. Jesus offered it as an example of how a person ought to pray. Before he gave the sample words though, He gave some instructions about the type of attitude we should have when we pray. In Mathew 6:5-6, Jesus said:

"And when you pray, do not be like the hypocrites, for they love to pray standing in the synagogues and on the street corners to be seen by others … But when you pray, go into your room, close the door and pray to your Father, who is unseen. Then your Father, who sees what is done in secret, will reward you."

Jesus makes the point that our prayers are between us and God. They are a private matter. They are not to be exploited as a means of drawing attention. Prayer is real communication with a real God. The act of praying privately is itself an act of faith. It requires a belief that God is a real and living God who knows us, hears our prayers, and is able to answer them. Were these beliefs not in place, it would be an act of foolishness to kneel privately behind closed doors, uttering words.

Jesus gave further instructions in the next few verses. I like the way it reads in the New American Standard Bible. "And when you are praying, do not use meaningless repetition as the Gentiles do, for they suppose that they will be heard for their many words. So, do not be like them; for your Father knows what you need before you ask Him." Some people interpret this verse to mean that we should keep our prayers short. I disagree. The Bible reveals many instances where people prayed for days. Nehemiah, as you may recall from Nehemiah 1:6, prayed day and night. In Esther 4:16, Queen Esther asked that the people fast with her for three days before she went in to see the king. It is assumed that the people prayed for those three days too because prayer is almost always associated with fasting in the Old Testament.

Actually, what Jesus said was not to use meaningless words like the Gentiles did, what some translations call babble. I suggest Jesus' point is the importance of a genuine faith in the living God when one prays, the kind of faith that realizes God is so intimate with us He knows what we need before we ask Him. This type of prayer contrasts meaningless words recited by a person with an unbelieving heart.

Notice Jesus did not follow his comment with instructions not to pray. Instead, He followed with a sample prayer. The fact that Jesus tells us God already knows what we need yet provides instructions on how to pray drives home the importance of the act of praying. We gain value in the asking, not because we are able to give God any new information, but because prayer acknowledges God as the one in control of our lives, our world, and all that exists. The value is also in the fact that prayer is the avenue for communing with the omnipotent, awesome God, and one of the means He has ordained for bringing about His perfect will.

The Lord's Prayer

In verses 9-13 of Mathew 6, we find Christ's sample prayer. Jesus begins the prayer with the words, "Our Father, who is in heaven." Jesus too models the practice of addressing prayers to God, the Father. Then He says, "Hallowed be Your name." Again, Jesus is teaching a truth we have seen before—God is holy.

Next, Jesus says, "Your kingdom come, your will be done on earth as it is in heaven." This interesting passage seems to imply that in heaven, or in the spiritual realm, God's will is done, whereas on earth, or in the fleshly realm, it is not, thus, the need to pray for it to be done on earth, too. Such an interpretation would further imply that God needs our help by means of our prayers in order to get this rebellious world under His control. This is not true at all!

The tool used for interpreting Scripture is always other Scripture. We understand Scripture by holding it in the light of the rest of Scripture. Using this method, we can quickly see that such an understanding of this verse cannot be correct. We know, for instance, that the spiritual realm in Biblical times and even today has warfare. The passage in Daniel 10 mentioned earlier is just one of many examples. Also, God does not need our help to accomplish anything. Mordicai advised Queen Esther in Esther 4:14, "If you remain silent at this time, relief and deliverance will arise … from another place." God will do what God will do with help from no one if He so chooses.

Isaiah 59:15-16, a passage we have looked at before, makes this point well:

"The Lord looked and was displeased that there was no justice. He saw that there was no one, he was appalled that there was no one to intervene; so his own arm achieved salvation ..."

What was Jesus trying to tell us about how we should pray? Personally, I think the words "Thy will be done on earth as it is in heaven" refers to the plans made by God before He laid the foundation of the world. Our prayers are a means for bringing about these plans. References to these plans can be found in many places in the Scriptures. Here are a few:

"For in perfect faithfulness you have done wonderful things, things planned long ago" (Isaiah 25:1).

"I am God, and there is none like me. I make known the end from the beginning, from ancient times, what is still to come. I say, 'My purpose will be stand ... What I have said, that I will bring about; what I have planned, that I will do" (Isaiah 46:9-11).

"But the plans of the Lord stand firm forever, the purpose of his love through all generations" (Psalm 33:11).

"The plan of the Holy One of Israel—let it approach, let it come into view, so we may know it" (Isaiah 5:19).

These plans are general in nature affecting nations as seen in Isaiah 14:26, "the plan determined for the whole world." These general plans can be seen throughout the Old Testament in the various prophecies about the nations, many of which have already been fulfilled.

In addition, God's plans are also specific for the lives of individuals. We can see the specificity of God's plans in the following:

"Before I formed you in the womb I knew you, before you were born I set you apart; I appointed you as a prophet to the nations" (Jeremiah 1:5).

"'I know the plans I have for you,' declares the Lord, 'plans to prosper you and not to harm you, plans to give you hope and a future'" (Jeremiah 29:11).

"Now when David had served God's purpose in his generation, he fell asleep" (Acts 13:36).

It is reassuring to know God has a purpose in every generation. Ephesians 1:11 assures us, "In him we were also chosen, having been predestined according to the plan of him who works out everything in conformity with the purpose of his will."

Sometimes, God's plans seem harsh and we have trouble understanding them. I have experienced many such times. Job certainly experienced it too. Job 23:14 says, "He carries out his decrees against me, and many such plans he still has in store." Jeremiah, known as the weeping prophet, echoed a similar theme when he said in Jeremiah 10:19, 23-24, "Woe to me because of my injury! My wound is incurable … Lord, I know that people's lives are not their own; it is not for them to direct their steps. Discipline me, Lord, but only in due measure—not in your anger, or you will reduce me to nothing."

In other passages, too, we see where God has planned harsh things for the wicked nations at the end of time. Revelation 17:17 says, "For God has put it into their hearts to accomplish his purpose by agreeing to hand over to the beast their royal authority, until God's words are fulfilled." Even with regards to Christ, Acts 2:23 tells us, "This man was handed over to you by God's deliberate plan and foreknowledge, and you, with the help of wicked men, put him to death by nailing him to the cross."

A few more verses make this point including Proverbs 16:9, which says, "In their hearts humans plan their course, but the Lord establishes their steps." Proverbs 16:4 says, "The Lord has made everything for its purpose, even the wicked for the day of trouble" (ESV).

God's plan *will* come about. Job 42:2 tells us no plan of God's can be thwarted. On the contrary, according to Romans 9:11-15, God thwarts the plans of the wicked. This point is made again in Acts 5:38-39 (ESV) where it says, "If this plan or this undertaking is of man, it will fail; but if it is of God, you will not be able to overthrow them."

Some New Testament prayer warriors use this understanding of God's absolute sovereignty. In Acts 4:24-28, Peter and John pray along with some of the early Christians and they recall in their prayer the fact that God had gathered together people to come against Jesus and to do whatever God's hand had predestined to occur. Paul remembers this truth in his prayers as well. In Romans 1:10, he uses it as a basis on which to petition God. Paul writes that he has been asking that, by God's will, he may somehow succeed in coming to them.

Such an understanding of God's sovereign will and purposes brings with it some natural questions. What about human free-will and our responsibility for our sins, for instance? This question could be a topic for a book all by itself. I shall not attempt to answer, except to pass on the opinion of a far more brilliant and learned mind than my own. Charles Hadley Spurgeon once wrote, "That God predestines, and yet that man is responsible, are two facts that few can see clearly ...

They are two lines that are so nearly parallel, that the human mind which pursues them farthest will never discover that they converge, but they do converge, and they will meet somewhere in eternity, close to the throne of God, whence all truth doth spring."[1]

Another question a belief in a sovereign God seems to ask is, "Why should we pray? Why is prayer necessary?" Since that question has been a pervasive theme in this book, hopefully, by now you know the answer. The great, awesome, and completely sovereign God has graciously included into His marvelous plan for the world some work that can be done by you and me. This work, when done faithfully, brings God's blessings upon us on earth and rewards stored up for us in heaven.

God's sovereign control over lives and our world is a far greater comfort than it is a distress. Because of this, believers can rejoice in all things. Rather than trying to make ourselves rejoice, it is clear that because God is in control of all things, if we are His, we *can* rejoice!

The next verse in the Lord's Prayer, Matthew 6:11, says, "Give us today our daily bread." For all those who might think the focus of our prayers should be only spiritual in nature and not physical, please note—Jesus included physical concerns in His model prayer. Our physical concerns are important to God. He wants us to ask Him for these, too.

Moving on to verse 12, Jesus said, "Forgive us our debts, as we also have forgiven our debtors." When I was a child and recited this prayer, I always assumed this verse meant something like this, "God please forgive my sins—always, all of them, every time I ask—and I will *try* to forgive other people who have sinned against me." In some ways, this assumption is true. First John 1:9 tells us that "If we confess our sins, he is faithful and just and will forgive us our sins and purify us from all unrighteousness." Micah 7:18-19 says, "Who is a God like you who pardons sin and forgives the transgression of the remnant of his inheritance? You do not stay angry forever but delight to show mercy. You will again have compassion on us; you will tread our sins underfoot and hurl our iniquities into the depths of the sea."

So, yes, God does forgive our sins when we confess them and ask for forgiveness. However, I think the second part of Mathew 6:12 is more than Jesus saying, "Oh, by the way, since God is so kind to forgive you, could you try your best to extend the favor by forgiving others?" The seriousness of our responsibility to forgive others can be found just a few verses down in this same chapter of Matthew. In Matthew 6:14-15 Jesus says, "For if you forgive other people when they sin against you, your heavenly Father will forgive you. But if you do not forgive others their sins, your Father will not forgive your sins."

The next line in Christ's model prayer, Matthew 6:13, says, "Lead us not into temptation, but deliver us from the evil one." Some manuscripts simply say evil instead of using the term "the evil one."

This is an interesting verse. Another verse helps us understand God's role in temptation. James 1:13 says, "When tempted, no one should say, 'God is tempting me.' For God cannot be tempted by evil, nor does he tempt anyone." Regarding the nature of temptation 1 Corinthians 10:13 says, "No temptation has overtaken you except what is common to mankind. And God is faithful; he will not let you be tempted beyond what you can bear. But when you are tempted, he will also provide a way out so that you can endure it."

In terms of God's ability to deliver us from the evil one, we should remember what 1 John 4:4 tells us—that the One who is in us, referring to the Holy Spirit who was given to all believers, is greater than the one who is in the world.

No, God does not tempt us, yet Jesus' words indicate that He can keep us from being led into temptation. Consistent with the understanding of God as sovereign, it is appropriate, and even modeled by Jesus, to petition God not to lead us into temptation but rather to deliver us from evil and the evil one. Throughout the Bible, we read examples of God delivering His children from evil. These examples are too numerous to list.

Often quoted as the last part of the Lord's Prayer is, "For Yours is the kingdom, the power and the glory, forever, Amen." This line can be found in Mathew 6:13 of some manuscripts. However, it is omitted in others, which explains why some churches and denominations recite this line while others do not. Whether Jesus actually uttered this last line is unclear. Nevertheless, it certainly would be appropriate in our prayers to remember and to state before God that all power and all glory are His forever.

Likewise, the word "Amen" may, or may not, have actually been uttered by Christ. Universally used today to end our prayers, amen is a Hebrew word that means certainly or verily.[2] Ending prayers with "Amen" signifies our agreement with what has been prayed. The word shows up in other places in Scripture. We see it in Deuteronomy 27 where the people say "Amen" many times after God's truth is spoken. David used it in Psalm 41:13 and Paul used it often in his writings. Amen also happens to be the last word in the Bible. What a fitting way for God's word to conclude.

Other Prayers of Jesus

Other than the model prayer, the Scriptures record many additional instances of Jesus praying. Prayer was an active part of Jesus' life. It was routine to Him rather than occasional. Numerous instances of Jesus going off by Himself to pray can be found in the Scripture including:

"After he had dismissed them, he went up on a mountainside by himself to pray" (Matthew 14:23).

"… went out to the mountainside to pray, and spent the night in prayer to God" (Luke 6:12 NASB). Some versions say that he spent the whole night praying to God.

This verse amazes me. I'm so tired at night that I don't think I am capable of spending a whole night in prayer! This passage reminds me of something that happened in the life of one of my friends many years ago. One evening my friend's husband came home from work and told her he did not love her any more, he was having an affair with another woman, and he wanted a divorce. This happened on April Fools' Day, but it was no joke.

After telling my friend this, he walked out of their house, leaving her alone with their two small children. She called another friend of mine named Judy. Judy's husband was out of town, so Judy took her little boy and went to our mutual friend's house to comfort her. The woman whose husband left had a small house with only two bedrooms. The two women put all of the children in one bedroom and shared the other one.

My friend told me later it was an extremely difficult night for her. She tossed and turned all night waking up many times. Every time she woke up, she saw Judy kneeling at the foot of the bed praying—all night long! I have been humbled by this image many times. I must confess that if my friend had called me instead of Judy that night I would have responded a little differently. I would have prayed with her. I might have even spent the night with her. But that's where the similarities end. I know I would not have been able to spend the whole night in prayer, like Judy did. If I am honest, I know I would not have stayed on my knees by my friend's bed all night long. God eventually healed my friend's marriage. It took time and much effort but my friend and her husband were finally reconciled. That was many years ago and they are still happily together today. In looking back, I can't help but think that Judy's all night prayers on the first night my friend heard the bad news must have opened the way for God's mighty healing power.

The day after Jesus' night in prayer, He chose his disciples. This illustrates another application of prayer. Before we take an action, especially one of spiritual importance, we should spend time in prayer. In addition to these times, Luke 9:28 -32 records Jesus praying with three of His disciples.

"About eight days after ... he took along Peter, John and James with him and went up onto a mountain to pray. And as he was praying, the appearance of his face changed, and his clothes became as bright as a flash of lightning. Two men, Moses and Elijah, appeared in glorious splendor, talking with Jesus ... Peter and his companions were sleepy, but when they became fully awake, they saw his glory and the two men standing with him."

Ahh! The awesome power of prayer! These two passages in Luke reiterate the fact that Jesus had a practice of prayer as well as point to the importance and power of prayer.

Public Prayer

Along with the numerous times Jesus prayed alone, or with only a few people, there were also times when He prayed publicly. One example can be found in Matthew 11. In this chapter, Jesus was speaking to an audience. He had harsh words about the cities that had seen His miracles but had not repented. Then He spoke tenderly, inviting people to come to Him. Stuck in between these two exhortations is a small prayer.

In this prayer, found in Matthew 11:25-26, Jesus said, "I praise you, Father, Lord of heaven and earth, because you have hidden these things from the wise and learned, revealed them to little children. Yes, Father, for this is what you were pleased to do." Jesus inserted this little prayer so naturally. It is as if God was in the crowd, and Jesus turned to say a personal word to Him. This small prayer is conversational, indicating that Jesus had an ongoing dialogue with the Father at all times. We should follow His example. First Thessalonians tells us to pray continually. Conversational prayers to God throughout the day are one way of doing this.

John 11:41-42 records another of Jesus' public prayers, made just prior to raising Lazarus from the dead. These verses say, "And so they took away the stone. Then Jesus looked up and said, 'Father, I thank you that you have heard me. I knew that you always hear me, but I said this for the benefit of the people standing here, that they may believe that you sent me.'"

Jesus made it clear in these verses that sometimes when we pray publicly our prayers are a witness to those around us. This passage is not in conflict with Matthew 6:5 where Jesus criticized praying in public. In that passage, Jesus criticized the use of public prayer as a self-serving tool for bringing attention to one's self. The problem in the verse was not that the prayer was made in public; the problem was the focus of the prayer. We must be careful to make sure our public prayers are for the purpose of being a public witness for the Lord, to make a public and joint petition to Him, or to bring public praise to Him.

Still another question arises with regards to the issue of praying publicly. Does public prayer contradict the teaching of Jesus in Matthew 6:6 where He says to "go into your room, close the door and pray to your Father who is unseen." These instructions to pray in private, along with Jesus' many examples of his own private prayer, are not in contradiction to His public prayers. Rather, these Scriptures validate both types of prayers. However, it should be noted that with public prayers comes the caution to keep the focus on God. Public prayers are not to be used as opportunities to draw attention to the one praying instead of to God.

Perhaps the longest, and in my opinion one of the most beautiful, of Jesus' prayers is recorded in the seventeenth chapter of John. This passage was spoken by Jesus to His disciples just after His last supper with them. The first part of the prayer is Jesus' personal conversation with God:

"After Jesus said this, he looked toward heaven, and prayed:
'Father, the hour has come. Glorify your Son, that the Son may glorify you. For you granted him authority over all people that he might give eternal life to all those you have given him. Now this is eternal life: that they know you, the only true God, and Jesus Christ, whom you have sent. I have brought you glory on earth by finishing the work you gave me to do. And now, Father, glorify me in your presence with

the glory I had with you before the world began.

I have revealed you to those whom you gave me out of the world. They were yours; you gave them to me and they have obeyed your word. Now they know that everything you have given me comes from you. For I gave them the words you gave me and they accepted them. They knew with certainty that I come from you, and they believed that you sent me."

Jesus prepared Himself for His final ministry, His upcoming death on the cross. Being God, Jesus knew the plan. He was discussing with the Father the fact that He had carried out God's will, thus far. He looked past the cross to what He knew waited for Him as He said in verse 5, "Glorify me in your presence with the glory I had with you before the world began." The writer of Hebrews makes mention of this point in Hebrews 12:2, "For the joy that was set before him he endured the cross, scorning its shame, and sat down at the right hand of the throne of God." What a blessing it is to have these words of Jesus recorded for us and what an honor to be privy to Jesus' personal conversation with His Father!

In the next few verses, Jesus prayed for the early Christians, those who were living in His day. Even with the ordeal of the cross ahead of Him, Jesus' concern was for His followers. This can be seen in John 17:9-15 where Jesus said, "I pray for them. I am not praying for the world, but for those you have given me, for they are yours. All I have is yours and all you have is mine. And glory has come to me through them" (verses 9-10).

What an awesome responsibility we have, we glorify Christ!

"I will remain in the world no longer, but they are still in the world, and I am coming to you. Holy Father, protect them by the power of your name, the name you gave me, so that they may be one as we are one. While I was with them, I protected them" (verses 11-12).

This is an interesting statement. How did Jesus guard His followers? He did not physically guard them. No, He guarded them spiritually through his teachings and his ministry ... and of course, through His prayers.

"I protected them and kept them safe ... None has been lost except the one doomed to destruction so that the Scripture would be fulfilled. I am coming to you now, but I say these things while I am still in the world, so that they may have the full measure of my joy within them. I have given them your word and the world has hated them, for they are not of the world any more than I am of the world" (verses 12-14).

Hebrews 11:38 calls Christ's followers people of whom the world was not worthy.

"My prayer is not that you take them out of the world but that you keep them from the evil one."

This is the second time Jesus asked the Father to keep his followers from the evil one, so it must have been important to Him. Why? What can the evil one do to the followers of Christ? We know that he cannot claim our souls. Jesus gave us this assurance in John 10:29 when he said, "No one can snatch them out of my Father's hand."

So what exactly can the evil one do to the followers of Jesus Christ? Actually, there is a lot he can do. He can bring evil upon us such as illness, accidents, or natural disasters. The evil one does this all the time. In addition, he also tempts us into sin in an effort to destroy our testimonies and rob us of our joy. When we see a fellow Christian fall into sin, we need to realize that he or she is under attack from an enemy whom Jesus called the evil one—not just *an* evil one but *the* evil one—the embodiment of all evil. We should reach out to such a fellow believer in love as we would a fallen comrade on the battlefield. Yet, all too often Christian groups or churches ostracize and push away the Christian who has sinned instead of dealing gently with the wayward, knowing that we ourselves are also beset with wickedness as it says in Hebrews 5:2.

I once knew a young minister who loved the Lord and had been used mightily of God to touch the lives of many for the cause of Christ. One of the people he helped was my own child. He spoke truth to my child at a critical time in her life. I am forever grateful to God for the way He used this man in my child's life.

However, this man was human and he fell into a sin area of his own. As is so often the case the man's situation was complicated and stemmed from hurt in his life. In spite of his failures, his heart continued to love the Lord. Even so, the Christian community around him closed ranks against him. The church he was a member of refused his request for counseling. This man was broken. He feared he would never be able to be used of God again and that was his heart's one desire and his life's greatest joy.

Fortunately, he served a faithful God who Psalm 34:18 says "is close to the brokenhearted and saves those who are crushed in spirit." A God who "heals the brokenhearted and binds up their wounds" according to Psalm 147:3. A God who 2 Samuel 14:14 tells us, "devises ways so that the banished person does not remain banished." In His faithfulness, God provided a few courageous and godly friends for this man, who prayed with him and helped him put his life back together.

I want to linger on this point a little longer because this type of judgmental and fraudulently pious reaction towards a fellow Christian in sin is all too common. Christians seem to forget that in the Scripture, it is Satan, the one Jesus called the evil one, who is referred to as the accuser of the brethren in Revelation 12:10. Job 2 tells us that he (Satan) stands before God day and night accusing the brethren. Maybe in Job's case the accusations were false but I am quite sure in most cases there are many accusations the evil one makes about God's people that are true. But God's people, sinful though we may be, are loved by Him. Zechariah 2:8 says we are "the apple of His eye." Isaiah 49:16 says our names are written on the palms of His hands, and of course, Jesus died for us!

We are still prone to committing sins; we will be so inclined until we die and are finally free from our fleshly bodies and this fallen world. When viewed from that perspective, how dare we judge as guilty whom God has judged as righteous. Of course, there's a place for godly discernment for the purpose of restoring the fallen brother, and protecting others from the harmful effects of sin. But to refuse to accept another's contrite heart is not a position that can be backed by Scripture.

On the contrary, Galatians 6:1 says, "If someone is caught in a sin, you who live by the Spirit should restore that person gently." To quote a friend, "If someone is not saved and they sin, we give them the cross. But if a person is a Christian, we hand them accountability. I want the cross. Please, give me the cross! The cross is for Christians, too."[3] Indeed, entrapping someone in his own sin is a huge tactic of the evil one. We need to remember always that the world we are in is enemy territory. We should follow this example of Jesus and ask God to protect us, and our fellow believers, from the evil one.

Let's examine John 17:20-26.

"My prayer is not for them alone. I pray also for those who will believe in me through their message, that all of them may be one, Father, just as you are in me and I am in you. May they also be in us so that the world may believe that you have sent me. I have given them the glory that you gave me, that they may be one as we are one—I in them and you in me—so that they may be brought to complete unity. Then the world will know that you sent me and have loved them even as you have loved me" (20-23).

These verses make it clear how important it is for us to love one another and be one in spirit with other believers. Twice Jesus says that our being one with each other, and one with God, is how an unbelieving world will know that God has sent Him. Similarly, at another time, John 13:35 recorded, Jesus saying, "By this everyone will know that you are my disciples, if you love for one another."

Continuing in the verses from John 17, Jesus says, "Father, I want those you have given me to be with me where I am, and to see my glory, the glory you have given me because you loved me before the creation of the world. Righteous Father, though the world does not know you, I know you, and they know that you have sent me. I have made you known to them, and will continue to make you known in order that the love you have for me may be in them, and that I myself may be in them" (verses 24-26).

In these verses, Jesus prays for the believers who will believe— those yet to come. *Jesus was praying for us*, for you and me! Jesus prayed for us just before His excruciating ordeal on the cross. That truth is almost too marvelous for words.

Jesus' primary concern is that we, His followers, become one with Him and one with each other, and that we share in His Father's love so others will know God sent Him. In other words, Jesus prays that we know and experience the gospel.

Jesus' Prayer for Peter

Before moving on to Christ's prayers in the Garden of Gethsemane and at Calvary, I want to mention one other time when Jesus prayed for someone. Luke 22:31-32 offers additional information about what was said by Jesus at the last supper when Jesus said to Peter, "Simon, Simon, Satan has asked to sift all of you as wheat. But I have prayed for you, Simon, that your faith may not fail. And when you have turned back, strengthen your brothers."

This is reminiscent of Job 1:6-12 where Satan asked permission to bring harm to Job. In both cases, Satan could do nothing without God's permission. But in both cases, permission was granted. The object of Satan's harassment both times was one of God's own. In the Luke passage, we see Jesus interceding for Peter through prayer. It is interesting to note that Jesus' intercession did not take the form of requesting God to not let Peter fail in the physical realm. Rather, Jesus asked God not to let Peter's *faith* fail. We know from the rest of the Gospels that Peter did fail physically. With his words, Peter adamantly denied knowing Jesus. Surely Peter's faith wavered, but it did not fail!

The last instruction Jesus added was "when you have turned back, strengthen your brothers." Often God's purposes for His children are that they undergo periods of sifting. These may include fleshly failures, doubts, even sin, as well as other afflictions. God's purpose in allowing these times is often so that the person will later be able to strengthen others who are experiencing similar trials.

Gethsemane

Jesus' prayers in the Garden of Gethsemane are recorded in most of the Gospels. One example can be found in Luke 22:40-47:

"On reaching the place, he said to them, 'Pray that you will not fall into temptation.' He withdrew about a stone's throw beyond them, knelt down and prayed, 'Father, if you are willing, take this cup from me; yet not my will, but yours be done.' An angel appeared to him and strengthened Him. And being in anguish, he prayed more earnestly, and his sweat was like drops of blood falling to the ground.

When he rose from prayer and went back to the disciples, he found them asleep, exhausted from sorrow. 'Why are you sleeping?' he asked them. 'Get up and pray so that you will not fall into temptation.'

While he was still speaking a crowd came up, and the man who was called Judas ... was leading them."

The other Gospels include additional information about the prayers and events in the garden. Mathew adds that Jesus said to His disciples, "My soul is very overwhelmed with sorrow to the point of death."

In Mark 14:36, Jesus prayed, "Abba, Father ... everything is possible for you. Take this cup from me. Yet, not what I will but what you will."

The Gospel of John does not give as much detail about Christ's prayers in the garden but it does add other information about the events of that night. According to John 18:4-8, after Judas arrived with his band of soldiers, "Jesus, knowing all that was going to happen to him, went out and asked them, 'Who is it that you want?'

'Jesus of Nazareth,' they replied.

Jesus answered, 'I told you that I am he. If you are looking for me, then let these men go."

In looking at Jesus' prayers in the Garden of Gethsemane, it is evident He was in deep agony. His agony was so great He sweated drops of blood. Once when one of my sons was about four years old he had to get stitches in his forehead. While getting the stitches, he strained so hard as he cried and fought the ordeal, he broke small blood vessels around his eyes, which caused tiny pinpoint red dots to appear around both eyes. These lasted for several days. Yet, my son's level of stress and angst pales in comparison to the agony Jesus experienced at Gethsemane. Jesus sweated drops of blood. His soul was overwhelmed with sorrow. Jesus did not say He was afraid, He said He was sorrowful. It was not his mind or heart that was sorrowful, it was his soul. He begged God to take the cup from Him. Why? What was it that made his soul so full of sorrow?

What loomed before Jesus was the greatest battle ever fought. Although it had a flesh and blood component, which would have been grueling all on its own, the real battle was spiritual against the powers of darkness. Ephesians 6:12 says, "For our struggle is not against flesh and blood, but against the rulers, against the authorities, against the powers of this dark world and against the spiritual forces of evil in the heavenly realms." The ordeal facing Jesus on Calvary was the ultimate war against these spiritual forces of evil in the heavenly realm. Jesus was about to be plunged into the deepest spiritual darkness ever known.

Yet, as grueling as the physical ordeal was going to be, and as dark and formidable as the forces of evil Jesus was about to face, what loomed greatest before Him was the overwhelming wrath of an angry God, *His* God, his beloved heavenly Father. The same Father who had descended in the form of a dove at Jesus' baptism in Matthew 3:17, and said of Him, "This is my Son, whom I love; with him I am well pleased." Soon this God, His God, would be furious with Him. Jesus was facing God's anger at its fullest force. Soon Jesus would have the sins of the world upon Him. And God hates sin!

This is what made Jesus' soul sorrowful. This was the plan and Jesus knew it. He was to become the object of God's wrath for all the sin that has ever or will ever occur, so that God's anger could be fully spent at the cross. Ever after, for those who follow Jesus, those who accept his gift of salvation, when God looks at them (at us) He does not see our sins. He sees instead the sacrifice His Son made on the cross. He sees the blood of His beloved Son, and He remembers His anger towards us was fully spent at the cross. He is angry no more and we are forgiven. Instead of seeing our sins, God sees us as His precious possession—so precious as to have been bought with the blood of His Son. Paul tells us in 2 Corinthians 5:21, "God made him who had no sin to be sin for us, so that in him we might become the righteousness of God."

Jesus was so distraught over the upcoming ordeal that He asked God to take the cup from Him. In making this request, Jesus modeled several important aspects of prayer. He modeled pouring one's heart out to God. In great agony, he begged God to change the plan. Jesus also modeled the importance of understanding God and knowing His nature. Jesus knew God was holy and just. He knew sin must be judged. Therefore, He also knew the only way God could take the cup from Him was to cancel His plan to save the souls of His creation. Consistent with His faithfulness, God answered Jesus' prayer. He gave Jesus an escape plan, leaving the decision to become the object of His angry judgment up to Jesus. God did not make Jesus do what He did. Jesus freely gave His life because of His great love for us.

In Matthew 26:52-54 Jesus said to the soldiers who were arresting Him, "Put your sword back into its place … Do you think I cannot call on my Father, and he will at once put at my disposal more than twelve legions of angels? But how then would the Scriptures be fulfilled that say it must happen this way?"

Finally, Jesus modeled the practice of yielding His will to God's no matter how difficult the path ahead may be. We see this when Jesus prayed, "'not as I will, but as you will'" (Matthew 26:39).

With renewed strength, Jesus faced the cross. He knew the physical ordeal ahead of Him. He knew the spiritual darkness he would face. He knew He was about to receive the full wrath of His heavenly Father. It was not easy for Him, but He knowingly left His throne in Glory and, undergirded by prayer, He was nailed willingly to a cross. So great was His love for you and for me!

Calvary

The narrative of Jesus' trial and crucifixion is recorded in all of the Gospels. The story of the crucifixion reads like this in Luke 23:26-49:

"As the soldiers led him away, they seized Simon of Cyrene, who was on his way in from the country, and put the cross on him and made him carry it behind Jesus. A large number of people followed him, including women who mourned and wailed for him. Jesus turned and said to them, 'Daughters of Jerusalem, do not weep for me; weep for yourselves and for your children ...'

Two other men, both criminals, were also led out with him to be executed. When they came to the place called the Skull, they crucified him there, along with the criminals—one on his right, the other on his left. Jesus said, 'Father, forgive them, for they do not know what they are doing.' And they divided up his clothes by casting lots.

The people stood watching, but the rulers even sneered at him. They said, 'He saved others; let him save himself ...'

The soldiers also came up and mocked him ...

There was also a written notice above him, which read: 'THIS IS THE KING OF THE JEWS.'

One of the criminals who hung there hurled insults at him: 'Aren't you the Messiah? Save yourself and us!'

But the other criminal rebuked him. 'Do you not fear God,' he said, 'since you are under the same sentence? We are punished justly, for we are getting what our deeds deserve. But this man has done nothing wrong.'

Then he said, 'Jesus, remember me when you come into your kingdom.'

Jesus answered him, 'Truly, I tell you, today you will be with me in Paradise.'

It was now about noon, and darkness came over the whole land until three in the afternoon ... And the curtain of the temple was torn in two. Jesus called out with a loud voice, 'Father, into your hands I commit my spirit.' When he said this, he breathed his last.

The centurion, seeing what had happened, praised God and said, 'Surely this was a righteous man.' ... But all those who knew him, including the women who had followed him from Galilee, stood at a distance, watching these things."

Keeping in mind that our definition of prayer is any words or thoughts directed to God, in these passages, we see two short prayers that Jesus uttered as he died. Verse 34 of this passage records Jesus saying, "Father, forgive them for they do not know what they are doing." Jesus was the ultimate intercessor. So great was his love for others that even as He was dying at their hands, he prayed for them. Hebrews 7:25 speaks of Jesus as an intercessor when it says, "Therefore he is able to save completely those who come to God through him, because He always lives to intercede for them."

The last of Jesus' prayers found in this passage (Luke 23:46) was spoken just before he died when Jesus said, "Father, into your hands I commit my spirit."

In order to gain greater perspective, and to better understand the extreme level of trust in God this prayer demonstrates, we need to be aware of another of Christ's prayers. Matthew 27:46 and Mark 15:34 tell us that Jesus said, "Eli, Eli, lema sabachthani?" which being translated means, "My God, my God, why have you forsaken me?"

When Jesus said these words, He was not just expressing his feelings of being forsaken, He also spoke an eternal truth. Jesus always spoke truth, and this was no exception because, at that moment, God had indeed forsaken Him. This truth is confirmed in other parts of Scripture. Habakkuk 1:13 says about God, "Your eyes are too pure to look on evil."

God is holy, a point made repeatedly in the Scriptures. A holy God does not coexist with evil. He conquers it, judges it, and casts it away from His presence. The first example of this was in Genesis 3:23 when God sent Adam and Eve out of the Garden of Eden away from His constant presence because they had sinned. God's holiness requires that He not have sin in His presence and the passage in Habakkuk lets us know God's nature will not even allow Him to look upon sin. This is the reason Jesus died, so that when God looks at us who are believers, God does not see our sin. Instead, God sees us cloaked in the righteousness of Christ, a righteousness bestowed upon us when we accept His gift of salvation.

So yes, God really did forsake Jesus as he hung on Calvary's cross. The crucifixion is prophesied in the book of Isaiah, chapters 52 and 53. The prophesy is completely accurate and was fulfilled at Jesus' death even to the smallest detail. For example, we find in Isaiah 53:7, "He was oppressed and afflicted, yet he did not open his mouth; he was led like a lamb to the slaughter ... he did not open his mouth." This verse was fulfilled in Luke 23:9 when Jesus was questioned by King Herod, at length, but He made no answer. In another example, Isaiah 53:9 says, "He was assigned a grave with the wicked, and with the rich in his death." Again, we know from the Gospels this was fulfilled. Jesus was crucified between two thieves yet he was buried in the tomb of a rich man named Joseph of Arimathea

Realizing then, that the prophecies in Isaiah 53 were literally fulfilled, it is important to notice other verses from Isaiah 53. Verses 9 and 10 say, "Though he had done no violence, nor was any deceit in his mouth. Yet it was the Lord's will to crush him."

God forsook Jesus. Jesus became sin for us and God turned His face away so as not to look upon sin. God crushed him. Understanding this puts some perspective on the depth of trust Jesus had in God when at the very moment God was forsaking him and crushing him, Jesus prayed, "Into your hands I commit my spirit."

Wow! In Isaiah 29:23 God says, "When they see … the works of my hands, they will keep my name holy … and will stand in awe of the God of Israel." When I think of what Christ did for me on the cross and how even as He was facing the worst ordeal ever known, He prayed for His enemies and trusted His God, it causes me to stand in awe! It also teaches me a tremendous amount about prayer.

QUESTIONS FOR REFLECTION

What did Jesus mean by His instruction not to recite meaningless words when we pray like the Gentiles did?

In Matthew 6:6, Jesus says to go into a room, shut the door, and pray in secret. Yet, at the same time, He models public prayer. Are these contradictions?

What is a caution regarding public prayer?

Why was Jesus sorrowful even to death at the Garden of Gethsemane? What loomed before Him there?

Yet, what did Jesus pray in this moment of agony?

What two amazing traits and behaviors, which we should imitate, did Jesus display on Calvary?

CHAPTER 11: PAUL

The apostle Paul is one of the most familiar prayer warriors in the Bible. A brilliant and educated man, he wrote most of the books in the New Testament: Romans, 1 and 2 Corinthians, Galatians, Ephesians, Philippians, Colossians, 1 and 2 Thessalonians, 1 and 2 Timothy, Titus, and Philemon. In addition, he is also listed among the possible writers of Hebrews.

Paul states his Jewish pedigree in Philippians 3:5, claiming he was circumcised the eighth day, an Israelite, of the tribe of Benjamin, a Hebrew of Hebrews, and a Pharisee. We learn in Philippians 3:6 that Paul persecuted the church with zeal. Present at the stoning of Stephen, the first Christian martyr, Paul was in hearty agreement with putting Stephen to death, according to Acts 8:1.

Then something happened to Paul, whose name had been Saul before his conversion, that changed his life and the course of history forever. He met Jesus. The story of Paul's encounter with Jesus is found in the ninth chapter of Acts. As Saul, as he was known then, traveled to the city of Damascus, a light from heaven flashed around him and he fell to the ground. He heard a voice call his name. Paul asked who was speaking, and the voice answered, "I am Jesus, whom you are persecuting." The men around Saul also heard the voice but they did not see the bright light that blinded Paul. For the next three days, Paul was blind and did not eat or drink anything.

Paul's conversion brought about a major change in his life, causing this man who had once thought highly of himself to write in 1

Timothy 1:15, "Christ Jesus came into the world to save sinners—of whom I am the worst" and in Philippians 3:7-8, "But whatever were gains to me I now consider loss for the sake of Christ. What is more, I consider everything a loss because of the surpassing worth of knowing Christ Jesus my Lord."

In his writings, Paul mentions prayer often, many times mentioning specific concerns. His prayers are more focused on eternal things than physical ones. It is Paul, after all, who exhorts us in 2 Corinthians 4:18 to "fix our eyes not on what is seen, but on what is unseen, since what we see is temporary, but what is unseen is eternal."

Because of this eternal focus, believers often site Paul's prayers as examples of how a person should pray, sometimes even implying this type of prayer is more proper or is of greater value than prayers about physical needs. I would argue otherwise. I believe Paul's prayers are indeed examples to be followed, but rather than showing a better way to pray, I think they simply show us *another* way to pray. They help to complete our understanding of prayer.

God is so much grander than we are. He is infinite while we are finite. Isaiah 55:9 says His ways are higher than our ways. Yet, God made us to be flesh and blood and to live in a tangible, physical world. We should earnestly pray about eternal issues as Paul did, but not at the neglect of the physical ones. Remember, Jesus himself taught us to ask for our daily bread when we pray.

When looking at Paul's prayers, it may be helpful to consider the unique circumstances of Paul's life in order to better understand his close relationship with Jesus Christ. Paul had no spouse or children. He walked with the Lord in ways no one else ever has, before or since. Unlike the men of the Old Testament, Paul interacted with the person of Jesus Christ. Yet unlike the disciples of the New Testament who knew Jesus while he was still in the flesh, Paul knew the risen Christ. Actually, Paul's encounter was with the glorified Christ as it came after Jesus' ascension into Heaven. Because of this, Paul is able to describe Jesus with some of the most beautiful words in the Bible. An example of such a description can be found in Colossians 1:14-20 where Paul describes Jesus as the One, "in whom we have redemption, the forgiveness of sins. The Son is the image of the invisible God, the firstborn over all creation. For in him all things were created: things in heaven and on earth, visible and invisible ... in him all things hold together ... making peace through his blood, shed on the cross."

Like Paul, our most significant relationship is our relationship with Jesus. Even so, we ought to be cognizant of, and diligently pray for, the other relationships in our lives, too. Paul never had to pray for a child in the hospital who was hanging on to life by a thread. I am not saying this to be critical of Paul. I am only pointing out that God has a role for each of us. God intended Paul to be exactly who he was, a man unencumbered by a family of his own in order that God might reveal Himself to Paul in unique and personal ways, which those of us with family demands are often too distracted to see. But that does not make our roles as intercessors for our children or spouses wrong, or any less valuable.

Keeping Paul's background information in mind, let's see the kinds of concerns Paul brought to the Lord in prayer.

Paul's Prayers

Paul's prayers, like his other writings, are filled with thanksgiving. This can be seen in the following passages:

"Thanks be to God ... through Jesus Christ our Lord!" (Romans 7:25).

"But thanks be to God! He gives us the victory through our Lord Jesus Christ" (1 Corinthians 15:57).

"Thanks be to God for his indescribable gift!" (2 Corinthians 9:15).

"Always giving thanks to God the Father for everything, in the name of our Lord Jesus Christ" (Ephesians 5:20).

"We always thank God, the Father of our Lord Jesus Christ, when we pray for you" (Colossians 1:3).

Paul offered thanks to God for the saints:

"We ought always to thanks to God for you, brothers and sisters ... because your faith is growing more and more, and the love all of you have for one another is increasing" (2 Thessalonians 1:3).

"How can we thank God enough for you in return for all the joy we have in the presence of our God because of you?" (1 Thessalonians 3:9).

"I have not stopped giving thanks for you, remembering you in my prayers" (Ephesians 1:16).

Like so many of the Biblical prayer warriors, Paul was careful to pray for God's will to be done. He understood that prayers not in line with God's will were futile. He made his petitions with this in mind. Evidence of this can be seen in the following passages:

"I remember you in my prayers at all times; and I pray that now at last by God's will the way may be opened for me to come to you"

(Romans 1:9-10).

"We constantly pray for you, that our God may make you worthy of his calling, and that by his power he may bring to fruition your every desire" (2 Thessalonians 1:11).

Paul's awareness of God's sovereign control and will is implicit in the previous verse. He asked God through His power to fulfill His will using the people for whom Paul was praying. Paul's belief in God's sovereign will can be seen in the way he began many of his letters. Ephesians, 1 and 2 Corinthians, Colossians, and 2 Timothy all begin with an acknowledgement of God's will.

Other than giving thanks and aligning with God's will, what were the specific things on Paul's heart when he prayed? What types of concerns did this godly man ask of God? As previously noted, Paul was always more concerned with the eternal than with the physical. He truly fixed his eyes on the Invisible One as he calls Jesus in Colossians 1:15. Because of this, Paul's prayers are some of the most beautiful in all of Scripture. Some examples of his prayers are:

"We constantly pray for you, that our God may make you worthy of his calling, and that by his power he may bring to fruition your every desire ... so that the name of our Lord Jesus may be glorified in you and you in Him" (2 Thessalonians 1:11-12).

"For this reason I kneel before the Father ... that out of his glorious riches he may strengthen you with power through his Spirit in your inner being, so that Christ may dwell in your hearts through faith. And I pray that you ... know this love that surpasses knowledge—that you may be filled to the measure of all the fullness of God" (Ephesians

3:14-19).

"Remembering you in my prayers ... that the God of our Lord Jesus Christ, the glorious Father, may give you the Spirit of wisdom ... that the eyes of your heart may be enlightened in order that you may know the hope to which he has called you, the riches of his glorious inheritance ... and his incomparable great power" (Ephesians 1:16-19).

"And this is my prayer: that your love may abound more and more in knowledge and depth of insight" (Philippians 1:9).

"We pray ... that you will not do anything wrong—not so that people will see that we have stood the test but so that you will do what is right even though we may seem to have failed," (2 Corinthians 13:7).

This verse is a personal favorite. No matter how my situation may appear to others, what's important is that I do what I know is right in God's eyes regardless of what others may think.

In addition, Paul occasionally prayed for physical needs. For example, Acts 28:8-9 tells of a time when Paul visited a man who was sick. Paul laid his hands on the man, prayed, and the man was healed. After this, many others came to Paul and were similarly healed.

Paul often asked others to pray for him, too. Some examples of this include:

"Pray also for me, that whenever I speak, words may be given me so that I will fearlessly make known the mystery of the gospel" (Ephesians 6:19).

"Join me in my struggle by praying to God for me. Pray that I be kept safe from the unbelievers in Judea ... so that I may come to you with joy, by God's will, and in your company be refreshed" (Romans

15:30-32).

"Pray for us that the message of the Lord may spread rapidly and be honored" (2 Thessalonians 3:1).

"Pray for us, too, that God may open a door for our message, so that we may proclaim the mystery of Christ" (Colossians 4:3).

"And pray that we may be delivered from wicked and evil people" (2 Thessalonians 3:2).

Paul's Teachings

Paul's writings include many teachings about prayer. Some of these principles have already been discussed in previous chapters. Because of this, Scripture containing these principles will be listed but not expounded upon in this chapter. Sometimes more than one teaching can be found in the same verse. Paul's various instructions often read like they are all part of the same larger lesson. The implication is that we need to try to incorporate them together with the goal of developing a more fruitful prayer life.

Joy and Thanksgiving

"Be joyful in hope, patient in affliction, faithful in prayer" (Romans 12:12).

"Rejoice in the Lord always. I will say it again: Rejoice!" (Philippians 4:4).

"I thank my God every time I remember you. In all my prayers for all of you, I always pray with joy" (Philippians 1:3-4).

"Pray continually, give thanks in all circumstances; for this is God's will for you in Christ Jesus" (1 Thessalonians 5:17-18).

"Devote yourselves to prayer, being watchful and thankful" (Colossians 4:2).

Perseverance

"The widow who is really in need and left all alone puts her hope in God and continues night and day to pray and ask God for help" (1 Timothy 5:5).

"Be ... faithful in prayer (Romans 12:12).

"And pray in the Spirit on all occasions with all kinds of prayers and requests. With this in mind, be alert and always keep on praying for all the Lord's people" (Ephesians 6:18).

"Pray continually" (1 Thessalonians 5:17).

Live Peacefully

"Be ... patient in affliction, faithful in prayer" (Romans 12:12).

"Therefore, I want the men everywhere to pray, lifting up holy hands without anger or disputing" (1 Timothy 2:8).

"Do not be anxious about anything, but in every situation, by prayer and petition, with thanksgiving, present your requests to God. And the peace of God, which transcends all understanding, will guard your hearts and your minds in Christ Jesus" (Philippians 4:6-7).

QUESTIONS FOR REFLECTION

What is the usual focus of Paul's prayers?

Is this a better way to pray?

What was especially unique about Paul's encounter with Jesus?

Chapter 12: Other Prayers in the New Testament

In the New Testament, the Holy Spirit descended upon multiple believers simultaneously on the day of Pentecost and continued to indwell them afterwards. This story can be found in Acts 2:3-4. From that day forward the Holy Spirit has been given to every believer at the time of their conversion and continues to indwell us until we die. Because of this, God's Spirit seems to pop up like popcorn all over the place, sometimes working through many people at the same time. With such an abundance of activity, in the New Testament we simply see recordings of people praying and the ways in which God responded to those prayers, instead of the actual words used. Some recorded instances of the disciples praying include:

"They all joined together constantly in prayer, along with the women and Mary the mother of Jesus, and with his brothers" (Acts 1:14).

"They devoted themselves to the apostles' teaching and to fellowship, to the breaking of bread, and to prayer" (Acts 2:42).

"So Peter was kept in prison, but the church was earnestly praying to God for him" (Acts 12:5).

"When it was time to leave, we left and continued on our way. All of them, including wives and children, accompanied us out of the city, and there on the beach, we knelt to pray" (Acts 21:5).

Zechariah

Although there are not as many recorded instances of specific prayer warriors and their prayers in the New Testament, there is one more that is worth mentioning. That prayer warrior is Zechariah, the father of John the Baptist. A study of the events surrounding the conception and birth of John the Baptist reveal some additional significant and interesting insights into the nature of prayer.

Luke 1 tells that Zechariah, the priest, received an answer to prayer when he learned of the upcoming birth of his child, the baby who was to become John the Baptist. While serving his priestly duties, with a multitude of people outside the temple praying, Zechariah burned incense to God inside the temple. An angel appeared to him and told him, in Luke 1:13-17, "Do not be afraid, Zechariah, for your prayer has been heard. Your wife Elizabeth will bear a son, and you are to call him John."

The angel then told him what the future would hold for the baby when he was grown, saying, "He will be great in the sight of the Lord … He will bring back many of the people of Israel to the Lord their God. And he will go on before the Lord, in the spirit and power of Elijah, to turn the hearts of the parents to their children and the disobedient to the wisdom of the righteous—to make ready a people prepared for the Lord."

We learn much about prayer from this story. Like Hannah and Samuel, we see again a baby who is a direct answer to prayer, but also a definite part of God's sovereign, pre-ordained plan for the world. This passage is one of the clearest examples of God's two-pronged work to both answer the heartfelt prayers of His people while simultaneously fulfilling His own divine purposes. Once again, my finite mind wants to entertain the questions: is God answering Zechariah's prayer, or is the announcement of John the Baptist's birth simply a fulfillment of a plan that was so obviously preordained as to have been prophesied in the book of Malachi?

Is John the Baptist's birth a direct result of Zechariah's prayers, implying that God does not work from a blueprint but rather acts somewhat impulsively in response to the prayers of people like Zechariah and Hannah? No, that *cannot* be the complete and accurate picture. The babies (John the Baptist and Samuel), whom God created in response to prayer, grow up to play too crucial a role in God's plans for their births to have been an impulsive response to their parent's pleas.

This way of thinking is dangerous. It would have us picturing God as a less than all-powerful being who must have been pleasantly surprised with the men John the Baptist and Samuel became. One proof this line of thinking is faulty is that John the Baptist's coming was foretold. The prophet Malachi said in Malachi 4:5-6, "See, I will send the prophet Elijah to you before the great and dreadful day of the Lord comes. He will turn the hearts of the parents to their children and the hearts of the children to their parents." Notice the similarity of the wording between this prophecy and what the angel told Zechariah? Certainly, it can be concluded that the birth of John the Baptist was preplanned and not only a result of prayer.

What is the answer then? Were the births and lives of Samuel and John the Baptist preplanned? If so, were the prayers of their parents necessary? As is so often the case in Scripture, even though they seem to contradict each other, both are correct. The evidence in Scripture plainly points to the fact that the births of these men were indeed preplanned, while at the same time the prayers of their parents were critically important.

I realize some do not find the idea that God is totally sovereign even to the smallest detail palatable, but Scripture is abundantly clear on this point. The seemingly paradoxical answer is that although God has preplanned and preordained the way things will go, prayer, or the lack of it, still plays a huge role! The angel in the Luke passage made this point in so many words when he said to Zechariah, "Your prayer has been heard." This statement indicates that preplanned as it may have been, the birth of John the Baptist was a direct answer to prayer just the same. The fact that God preplans yet our prayers are real, effective, and necessary, is a mystery and an amazing truth!

Another point derived from the interaction between Zechariah and the angel is that sometimes, and perhaps often, God's answers to our prayers do not come immediately or even quickly. Zechariah and his wife Elizabeth were old. Luke 1:6-7 says, "Both of them were righteous in the sight of God, observing all the Lord's commands and decrees blamelessly. But they were childless, because Elizabeth was not able to conceive and they were both very old."

Think about that for a minute. They were both very old. How long do you think Zechariah had been praying for a child? Do you think this was a new or even recent prayer? Some believe that since Zechariah was in the Temple praying when the angel told him his prayers had been heard, this request for a child must have been what he had been praying about. I have heard it taught that Zechariah was in the temple praying for a child and the angel came as a result.

I don't think that is the case at all. Scripture certainly does not tell us that. Zechariah was in the Temple burning incense while the people prayed outside. Zechariah was a priest. It was his routine duty to enter the Temple and burn incense to the Lord. I think it is far more likely that his prayers at that moment were for the people he served. It was, after all, his duty as priest to enter the Temple and make intercession for the people. He had done this faithfully for many years.

Personally, I do not think Zechariah prayed for a child that day. Quite likely, the prayer for a child was something he had prayed for at home with his wife Elizabeth, perhaps for many, many years. It is also possible that he, or they, had even stopped asking God for a child. They may have even assumed that since God had not blessed them with a child, that remaining childless was God's will for them. They had perhaps determined in their hearts to accept God's ruling on this matter, even though it was painful for them. But the angel told Zechariah that God had *heard* his prayer—a prayer that had possibly been made many years earlier.

Yet, the angel spoke as if the request was current. This offers some perspective on God's timing. God is not constrained by time as we are. Second Peter 3:8 tells us that to God, "A day is like a thousand years, and a thousand years are like a day." In His perfect timing, God answered Zechariah's prayer according to His perfect will for His purposes. In answering this prayer, God confirmed some of what Scripture teaches about God's nature and prayer. He gave Zechariah the desire of his heart, as Psalm 37:4 says He will, if we delight in Him. He heard Zechariah's prayer as 1 Peter 3:12 and other places in the Scripture say He does. Zechariah was a righteous man and his prayer was powerful and effective like James 5:16 tells us. All of this happened according to God's perfect will.

Prayers in the book of Revelation

In Revelation, the last book of the Bible, prayers are mentioned a couple of times. In both cases, there are some commonalities. In order to better see these it may be necessary to have an understanding of some aspects of the specific Scriptures we are considering.

First, it is important to remember that the book of Revelation is one of the most difficult books in the entire Bible to understand. Even so, as is always the case when dealing with Scripture, by comparing it to other Scripture we can gain at least some understanding of this difficult book.

Before reading the specific Revelation passages where prayers are mentioned, as background information, it should be noted that in other places in Scripture that God's presence was accompanied by lightening, peals of thunder, earthquakes, fire, smoke, and other bold signs. Some examples include:

"Mount Sinai was covered in smoke, because the Lord descended on it in fire. The smoke billowed up from it like smoke from a furnace, and the whole mountain trembled" (Exodus 19:18).

"Do you have an arm like God's, and can your voice thunder like his?" (Job 40:9).

"The Lord Almighty will come with thunder and earthquake and great noise, with windstorm and tempest and flames of a devouring fire" (Isaiah 29:6).

Understanding that God's presence, direct intervention, and sometimes even His judgments, are marked by bold signs, let's read two of the Revelation passages where prayer is mentioned.

Revelation 6:9-15: "When he opened the fifth seal, I saw under the

altar the souls of those who had been slain because of the word of God
… They called out in a loud voice, saying, 'How long, Sovereign Lord,
holy and true, until you judge the inhabitants of the earth and avenge
our blood? … I watched as he opened the sixth seal. There was a great
earthquake. The sun became black … the whole moon turned blood
red, and the stars in the sky fell to the earth … The heavens receded
like a scroll being rolled up, and every mountain and island was
removed from its place."

Revelation 8:3-5: "Another angel, who had a golden censer, came
and stood at the altar. He was given much incense to offer, with the
prayers of all God's people on the golden altar in front of the throne.
The smoke of the incense, together with the prayers of God's people
went up before God from the angel's hand. Then the angel took the
censer, filled it with fire from the altar, and hurled it on the earth; and
there came peals of thunder, rumblings, flashes of lightening and an
earthquake."

These are powerful images. They are in some ways the most vivid
description of the power of prayer recorded anywhere in Scripture. In
both cases, we see the prayers of God's people. In one of the cases, the
prayers have been collected into golden censers and in the other, the
souls of the saints themselves cry out to God. In both cases, God
appears moved to action by these prayers. In both cases, prayers
precede dramatic activity by God.

QUESTIONS FOR REFLECTION

What is a basic difference in the way prayers are recorded in the Old Testament as opposed to the New Testament?

What two new insights do we gain from Zechariah's prayer for a child?

What truth about prayer is vividly portrayed in the book of Revelation?

Chapter 13: The Awesome Power of Prayer

"Is anyone among you in trouble? Let them pray. Is anyone happy? Let him sing songs of praise. Is anyone among you sick? Let them call the elders of the church to pray over them, and anoint them with oil in the name of the Lord. And the prayer offered in faith will make the sick person well; the Lord will raise them up. If they have sinned, they will be forgiven. Therefore, confess your sins to each other and pray for each other so that you may be healed. The prayer of a righteous person is powerful and effective

Elijah was a human being, even as we are. He prayed earnestly that it would not rain, and it did not rain on the land for three years. Again he prayed, and the heaven gave rain and the earth produced its crops" (James 5:13-18).

The awesome power of prayer! A study of the Scripture reveals the most amazing stories of God's glory revealed, people's lives changed, God's purposes fulfilled, great and marvelous things happening because of prayer. The following is a list of some of the occurrences in the Bible that came either right after, or simultaneously, with prayer.

Moses cried out to God, then God parted the waters of the Red Sea and the people safely crossed over on dry land (Exodus 14:15-21).

Samson prayed, asking God to give him strength one last time. After praying, he grasped the two middle pillars of a building that supported well over 3,000 people. Then he single-handedly pushed the pillars apart causing the building to collapse, killing all of the wicked people in it (Judges 16:26-31).

Hannah conceived Samuel after praying earnestly (1 Samuel 1:10-20).

Solomon prayed at the dedication of the temple of the Lord (1 Kings 8:22-61).

Elijah cried to the Lord and the widow's son was raised from the dead (1 Kings 17:20-22).

Elijah prayed, then God sent fire down from heaven when three hundred of Baal's priests could not get their god to respond to their prayers (1 Kings 18:36-38).

Elijah prayed and it did not rain for three and one half years. Then he prayed again and the rains came (James 5:17-18).

Elijah prayed and the Shumite woman's son came back to life (2 Kings 4:33-34).

Elijah prayed and the eyes of his servant were opened and the servant was able to see an army of angels with horses and chariots and fire all around standing between them and the invading Syrian army (2 Kings 6:17).

Hezekiah prayed asking God to save his nation from the Assyrian army. In answer to this prayer, "That night the angel of the Lord went out and put to death a hundred and eighty-five thousand in the Assyrian camp. When the people got up the next morning—there were all the dead bodies!" (2 Kings 19:35).

Hezekiah prayed and God worked two miracles:

1)   He healed Hezekiah, bringing him back from the brink of death, adding fifteen years to his life (2 Kings 20:5-6).

2)   As a sign He was going to do this miracle, God made the shadow cast by the declining sun on the dial of Ahaz turn back ten steps. In other words, God turned back time (Isaiah 38:8).

Nehemiah prayed and was able to successfully supervise the rebuilding of the wall of Jerusalem in spite of great opposition (Book of Nehemiah).

Esther led her people in observing three days of fasting and prayer (Esther 4:16), before being used by God as an instrument of salvation for her people (Esther Chapter 8).

The fortunes of Job were restored when he prayed for his friends (Job 42:10).

Daniel prayed three times a day, every day. Because of this, he was thrown into the lions' den but the lions did not harm him (Daniel 6).

Zechariah prayed and in response to his prayer, his wife Elizabeth conceived their son, John the Baptist (Luke 1:13).

Jesus began his ministry after first rising in the morning and praying (Mark 1:35-39).

Jesus prayed asking God to bless five loaves of bread and two fish He had, then used them to feed five thousand people. The people ate until they were full and there were twelve baskets full leftover (Mark 6:39-44).

Before Jesus walked on water to join his disciples in their boat, He had spent the afternoon on a mountain alone, praying (Mark 6:46-49).

Jesus offered a prayer of thanksgiving to God just before feeding four thousand people with seven loaves of bread and a few small fish.

There were seven baskets of food left over (Mark 8:6-9).

When Jesus' disciples were not able to cast a demon out of a boy, Jesus cast it out. Afterwards he told his disciples, "This kind [of demon] can only come out by prayer" (Mark 9:29, with author insertion).

Anna saw the Christ child after spending many, many years in prayer and fasting. She did not have to seek after him either, God brought the Christ child to her in the temple where she was (Luke 2:36-38).

When Jesus was being baptized, as He was praying the heavens were opened, the Holy Spirit descended on him like a dove, and a voice spoke from heaven saying "This is my beloved son in whom I am well pleased" (Luke 3:21-22).

Jesus chose the twelve disciples after first praying all day and all night (Luke 6:12-13).

The story of the transfiguration as recorded in Luke says that Jesus took Peter, John, and James with Him to the mountain to pray and as He prayed, the appearance of His face was altered and His clothing became dazzling white (Luke 9:28-29).

Just before raising Lazarus from the dead, Jesus lifted His eyes upward and prayed (John 11:41-44).

While Jesus was praying in the Garden of Gethsemane, God sent an angel to minister to Him (Luke 22:43).

After Jesus prayed earnestly in Gethsemane, He had the strength He needed to endure the cross (Luke 22:39-23:56).

In Acts 4:31 when the believers prayed, the place in which they were gathered shook, they were filled with the Holy Spirit and they continued to speak the word of God boldly.

After Paul had encountered Jesus on the road to Damascus, while he was still blind, God sent a vision to Ananias to come to him and restore his sight. Acts 9:11 tells us that when God told Ananias to go to Paul, He said, "Go to the house of Judas ... and ask for a man from Tarsus named Saul, for *he is praying*" (Acts 9:11).

Cornelius was not a Jew. He was a Roman Centurion. Yet, God sent Peter to explain salvation to him because he was a devout man who feared God and prayed continually to God. In a vision, an angel told Cornelius his prayers and alms had ascended as a memorial before God (Acts 10:1-8).

An angel led Peter out of prison past the Roman soldiers in the still of the night when earnest prayer for him was made to God by the churches (Acts 12:5).

Paul and Silas were in prison praying and singing hymns when suddenly a great earthquake shook the prison causing all of the doors to open and all of the chains to fall off of the prisoners (Acts 16:25-26).

John was in the Spirit on the Lord's Day, when he was given the revelation of what was to come in the end times. He was given this revelation by an angel. I am certain John was praying that day (Revelation 1:10).

Either God's word is true or it is not. If it is indeed true, as I believe it to be, then all of these things occurred accompanied by prayers which had been lifted up to the one, true, and omnipotent God by an effective prayer warrior.

CHAPTER 14: CONCLUSION

Prayer is my calling and my delight. I have spent years studying and practicing it. Some mysteries about prayer I still cannot explain or fully comprehend. Perhaps the greatest of these mysteries and the one I have the most trouble wrapping my brain around is how God is sovereign, yet prayer is still important. The understanding that God is completely sovereign, totally in control, and has a plan, seems to be diametrically opposed to the understanding that our prayers are valuable and even necessary. Because these concepts seem to run counter to each other, we are tempted with our finite minds to camp ourselves on one side. Sometimes we fall into believing that since God is in control of all things, we do not need to pray. This faulty position can cause us to be negligent in our responsibility to pray. Remember the words of Samuel in 1 Samuel 12:23, "As for me, far be it from me that I should sin against the Lord by failing to pray for you."

Other times we mistakenly think God cannot accomplish His will without our prayers. Underlying this position is the belief that our God is not all-powerful. Again, words of Scripture come to mind. Isaiah 59:15-16 says, "The Lord looked and was displeased that there was no justice. He saw that there was no one, he was appalled that there was no one to intervene; so his own arm achieved salvation." God *can* accomplish His will without our help and just as surely, we will miss a blessing if we do not allow ourselves to be used by Him.

Even if we still cannot fully understand it, I hope by now we at least realize both positions are simultaneously true. God is completely sovereign and all-powerful, and at the same time, our prayers are tremendously valuable. My goal in this book has been to increase your desire to pray and to equip you with an understanding of how to pray more effectively.

Another mystery that continues to give me pause is why it sometimes seems that our prayers are not answered. That question is multidimensional. As we have seen through the Scriptures, circumstances, attitudes, and actions such as sin, a lack of a personal walk with God, mistreatment of others, a haughty attitude, and many other things can interfere with our prayers. On the other hand, there are ways to enhance our effectiveness as prayer warriors. Some of these ways include humility, personal holiness, and a concern for others. In addition, sometimes there are spiritual interferences to our prayers such as we saw in the tenth chapter of Daniel. However, usually when it appears that God is not answering, He is actually either saying "no" to our petition like He did to Paul's request in 2 Corinthians 12:8-9 to have the thorn in his flesh removed, or He is saying "wait" like He did to Zechariah's prayer for a child in the first chapter of Luke.

As this study is brought to a conclusion, I will recap by reciting once again what an effective prayer warrior looks like, what his or her prayers sound like, under what circumstances he or she prays, where he or she prays, and who or what he or she prays about.

Who is a prayer warrior? What does he or she look like?

An effective prayer warrior is a Christian. In other words, she is a sinner like everyone who has ever lived, who has acknowledged those sins and realized the need for a solution to the sin problem. This person has therefore accepted God's gift of salvation by acknowledging an understanding that Jesus paid for those sins with His blood by His death on the cross. She has asked Jesus to forgive those sins and to become her personal savior. Because of the salvation experience, the person can come into God's presence in prayer cloaked in the righteousness of Christ as is spoken of in Philippians 3:9-10. We know from James 5:16 the prayers of the righteous are effective and powerful.

In addition to being saved, a prayer warrior communes with God through a regular practice of prayer and Bible study. He is concerned with maintaining his own personal holiness knowing that sin can interfere with his prayers as is stated in Psalm 66:18. He is quick to repent and confess his sins as James 5:16 instructs while at the same time, with the help of God, he demonstrates self-control, like 1 Peter 4:7 reminds. He has a great love and concern for others for whom he intercedes, and he yields his will to God's.

This person may be a man, woman, or child. We see all of these kneeling to pray in Acts 21:5. He may be single like Paul, according to 1 Corinthians 7:8, or married, like the people instructed about prayer in 1 Peter 3:7. He may pray alone as Jesus often did in Matthew 14:23, and many other times, or with others as the disciples did in Acts 1:13-14. He may be a king like Hezekiah or an average person like the disciples. He may be sick like James 5:13 speaks of, on his deathbed as Hezekiah was in Isaiah 38:1, or strong as were many in the Scripture. He may be guilty of sin like David was or not guilty of sin like Job. He may be joyful like the people worshiping in 1 Kings 1:40 or tormented like Job was in Job 10:1. He may be rich like King Solomon or destitute like Job and like David became for a while. He may be thanking God for a great victory in his life like David did in 1 Samuel 17:4 after killing Goliath, or asking for help in order to accept defeat like Habakkuk did in Habakkuk 3:16.

What do a prayer warrior's prayers sound like?

We covered this question at length in the chapter on Psalms. When desiring to know what the content of our prayers should be, there's no better place than Psalms to turn as demonstrated through the many, many prayers of King David and the other Psalmists. As a review, I will once again list the ten points covered in that chapter.

1)   Our prayers should be made to God the Father through the Son at the prompting and with the help of the Holy Spirit.

2)   Prayers are filled with praise and thanksgiving.

3)   We come humbly to God, confessing our sins, asking for forgiveness, and recognizing our personal unworthiness before God.

4)   We can petition God based on His character.

5)   We can petition God based on His promises.

6)   We can petition God based on His ability to answer our prayers.

7)   We can petition God based on His will.

8)   We can petition God based on His glory.

9)   We should recognize what He has done in our lives.

10)   We can pour out our hearts to Him as it says in Lamentations 2:19, "Pour out your heart like water before the presence of the Lord." This last point is sort of a catchall. It reminds us that we can actually pray to our Heavenly Father about anything that is on our hearts.

When does a prayer warrior pray?

According to Biblical precedent, an effective prayer warrior may pray anytime day or night. He may pray before something happens as Jesus did in Luke 6:12 before He chose His disciples and in John 17 before He faced the cross or after something happens like Jonah did in Jonah 2:1 after the whale swallowed him. He may pray before dawn like the psalmist in Psalm 119:147, in the morning like we see in Psalm 5:3, at noon like Peter did in Acts 10:9, in the afternoon like Cornelius in Acts 10:30, in the evening like Jesus in Matthew 14:23, or in the middle of the night like Jesus did in Luke 6:12. He can pray three times a day like Daniel in Daniel 6:10, day and night like Paul writes about in 1 Thessalonians 3:10, every day like is recorded in Psalm 88:9, always like Paul in Philippians 1:4, or continually like we are told to in 1 Thessalonians 5:16-18.

Where does a prayer warrior pray?

The Bible shows us that an effective prayer warrior may pray seemingly anywhere. The Bible tells us people were a variety of places when they prayed. Isaiah speaks of praying in a temple or church in Isaiah 56:7. A group of early believers prayed on a beach in Acts 21:5. Jesus prayed on a mountain in Luke 6:12. Paul and Silas prayed while in a jail cell in Acts 16:25. Jonah prayed from inside the belly of a whale in Jonah 2:1. Jesus often prayed from a desolate place but he instructed that we pray from our own room in our home in Matthew 6:6. Daniel prayed by a window in Daniel 6:10. Jesus prayed in a garden in John 18:1. The psalmist writes about praying from a bed in Psalm 149:5. Jesus prayed alone in Luke 22:41, with a few people in Luke 9:28, and with many in a public prayer in John 11:41-42.

How does a prayer warrior pray?

Again, according to Biblical examples, an effective prayer warrior may be found praying in a wide variety of ways. He may pray while kneeling like Ezra did in Ezra 9:5. He may pray while lying prostrate like Abraham did in Genesis 17:3. He could be on a bed like King Hezekiah in Isaiah 38:1, on the ground like David in 2 Samuel 12:16, or standing as Jesus instructed in Mark 11:25. A prayer warrior might have his eyes lifted towards heaven like Jesus did in John 17:1 or his eyes may be downcast like the tax collector in Jesus's parable in Luke 18:13. He may be praying with loud cries like Jesus did according to Hebrews 5:7 or he may be offering up a whispered prayer like is spoken of in Isaiah 26:16. He may even be praying so softly that his lips are moving but there is no sound coming from them like Hannah in 1 Samuel 1:13.

Any physical position is acceptable to the Lord when a person is praying. God sees our hearts when we pray.

Who or what does a prayer warrior pray for?

As we have seen throughout this book, there is a wide variety of answers to this question as well. In the Bible we find people praying for their children such as in Lamentations 2:19, for themselves like Paul did in 2 Corinthians 12:7-10, for their friends like Job did in Job 42:10, and for their possessions like Ezra did in Ezra 8:21. They pray for safe travel as Ezra also did in Ezra 8:21, for those who are who are sick or suffering like in James 5:13-14, for kings and people who are in high positions like Paul instructs in 1 Timothy 2:2, and for the saints as per Paul's instructions in Ephesians 6:18. In addition, Jesus instructed us to pray for our enemies and those who mistreat us in Luke 6:28. Actually,

Paul tells us clearly who we should pray for in 1 Timothy 2:1 when he writes, "I urge, then, first of all, that petitions, prayers, intercession and thanksgiving be made for all people." In terms of what should be prayed for, an effective prayer warrior prays for God's will to be done and His purposes be established.

The practice of prayer as explained in the Bible is like a multifaceted diamond. Each facet is intriguing and beautiful. Each facet can be illuminated and studied by itself. This is what I have endeavored to do in this book. Yet, if I was asked to make only one point about prayer, the point I would make would be that real prayer is God focused. It is about God, not about us. In prayer, we focus our eyes on God rather than trying to get Him to focus His eyes on us.

Admittedly, there are times when those praying in the Bible ask God to open His eyes and ears to their petitions as Nehemiah does in Nehemiah 1:6. Even though this is true, a thorough study of the Scripture will reveal that the essence of those prayers were an attempt to understand what God was doing in their lives and the lives of those they were praying for. Those prayers were also God focused.

God brought this point to me several years ago at a difficult time in my life. Someone I loved had become the victim of another person's sin. My friend struggled to survive in the aftermath of this incident. She had lost her sense of self-worth, her ability to trust others, and for a brief time, even her faith in God. I began praying more fervently than I had prayed ever before. I fasted. I wept. I begged God to help my friend. My prayers were completely focused on my friend and her plight.

At the same time, I was reading the Psalms in my daily devotions. One day it just hit me, like a light bulb going off in my head, David seldom appealed to God based on himself (his need or his trauma). He did sometimes tell God about his persecution or pain. Actually, he did this quite often, but seldom was it a basis for his petitions. Instead, most of the time David petitioned based on God Himself. It is true that occasionally he made petitions based on his needs. An example of this is Psalm 6:2 which reads, "Have mercy on me, Lord, for I am faint; help me, Lord, for my bones are in agony." More often though, David prayed words like the ones in Psalm 86:15-16, "But you, Lord, are a compassionate and gracious God, slow to anger, abounding in love and faithfulness. Turn to me and have mercy on me." Similarly, in Psalm 25:11, David used God focused words when he wrote, "For the sake of your name, Lord, forgive my iniquity, though it is great," and again in Psalm 44:26, "Rise up and help us; rescue us because of your unfailing love."

As I read verses like these, I realized that David often sounded like a lawyer arguing a case before a judge based on the law. For instance, in the verses cited above, David says to God, "You are gracious" and then a verse later, he says, "Be gracious to me." Doesn't that sound like a lawyer? The law says such and such, now apply that law to me. The "law" is that God is good, He is full of loving kindness, He pardons the sins of His people, and His hand is favorably disposed towards those who fear Him, etc.

Like a good lawyer arguing before a judge, when we come before God in our prayers, we too can stand on the law and precedents. The law, as I am calling it, does not refer to the law handed down by God in the Old Testament. Rather, I am speaking of all the truths about God that are spelled out in the Scriptures. Precedents are the promises of God and the ways He has acted in similar situations that we find in the

Scriptures.

This insight revolutionized my prayer life! I stopped asking God to help my friend because she was hurting. I began asking instead for God to help her because of His loving kindness and His tender mercies. I began asking for His favor in this situation for His own name's sake, and for His glory, instead of for her sake or for my comfort. I found that when I prayed this way, I came away from my prayer time encouraged and full of hope. This perspective gave me strength because I knew I was on solid Biblical ground in my requests. I have come to understand this is truly the correct perspective.

Prayer is not about me—it's all about God!

NOTES

Chapter 1: Why Pray?
1 — Charles Stanley, *When the Enemy Strike: The Keys to Winning your Spiritual Battles* (Nashville: Thomas Nelson, Inc., 2004), 71

Old Testament
1 — John Piper, *Desiring God: Meditations of a Christian Hedonist* (Colorado Springs: Multnomah Books, 1986, 1996, 2003), 171

Chapter 2: Moses
1 — Chaim Herzog & Mordechai Gighon, *Battles of the Bible: A Military History of Ancient Israel* (New York City: Barnes & Noble Publishing. Inc., by arrangement with Greenhill Books / Lionel Leventhal Ltd, 1978, 1997), 36
2 — T. Keith Edwards, MD, conversation, December 2004

Chapter 3: David / Psalms

David
1 — Kristin Michael, "The God of Good," Asbury College, Wilmore, KY 2005
2 — Charles Swindoll, *Laugh Again* (Nashville: W Publishing Group, 1992), 146.
3 — A. W. Tozer, *The Root of the Righteous* (Chicago: Moody Publishers, 1955, 1986), 165.
4 — Susan Anderson, *So This is Africa* (Nashville: Broadman Press, 1943), 128.

The Psalms
1 — Edwards T. Welch, *Depression a Stubborn Darkness: Light for the Path* (Winston-Salem: Punch Press, a series published in cooperation with The Christian Counseling and Educational Foundation Glenside, PA, 2004), 58
2 — [Susan] Siami, conversation, 2004

Chapter 4: Hannah, Samuel, Daniel, Nehemiah, Ezra, and Habakkuk

Nehemiah
1 — Susan Siami, conversation, 2007
2 — Susan Small, Christian Academy of Louisville prayer group, 2005

Ezra
1 — Susan Siami, conversation, 2006

Chapter 5: Abraham, Jacob, Hezekiah, Solomon, and Jehoshaphat

Jacob
1 — Dr. Adrian Rogers, *Love Worth Finding,* Radio Ministry, WFIA "the Spirit" Louisville, KY. 2007. Originally broadcast February 22, 1987.

Chapter 6: Job
1 — Edward T. Welch, *Depression a Stubborn Darkness: Light for the Path* (Winston-Salem: Punch Press a series published in cooperation with The Christian Counseling and Educational Foundation Glenside, PA, 2004) 83

Chapter 8: Teachings on Prayer

Strengthening Our Love
1 - D. A. Carson, *A Call to Spiritual Reformation: Priorities from Paul and His Prayer* (Grand Rapids: Baker Books and InterVarsity Press Nottingham, United Kingdom, 1992) 85
2 — John Miller, *Come Back, Barbara: Second Edition* (Phillipsburg: P&R Publishing, 1988, 1997) 150

Prayer is Work
1 — Susan Siami, Christian Academy of Louisville prayer group, 2006
2 — Deb Norris Edwards, conversation, 2006
3 — Susan Siami, conversation, 2006
4 —Chip Ingram, *The Invisible War: What Every Believer Needs to Know About Satan, Demons, and Spiritual Warfare* (Grand Rapids: Baker Books 2006) 160

Faith
1 — T. K. Edwards, MD —prayer meeting at Ogbomosho Baptist Hospital, Ogbomosho, Nigeria mid 1960's

Chapter 9: More Teachings on Prayer

Praise and Thanksgiving
1 — Funeral of Karen Lynn Noble, Bluefield, WV May 1978

The Content of Our Prayers
1 — *Webster's Ninth New Collegiate Dictionary* (Springfield: Merriam-Webster Inc., 1987)

2 — Adrian Rogers, *Love Worth Finding,* radio show WFIA "the Spirit" Louisville, KY. Originally broadcast February 22, 1987.

Chapter 10: Jesus
1 — Charles Hadley Spurgeon, *A Defense of Calvinism,* http://www.reformed.org/calvinism

2 — *Webster's Ninth New Collegiate Dictionary* (Merriam-Webster Inc., 1987)

3 — Susan Siami, conversation 2005

ABOUT THE AUTHOR

Born in Nigeria, West Africa, as the daughter of missionaries, Harriet Michael is a writer, gardener, wife of over 35 years, mother of four, and grandmother of one.

She holds a BS in nursing from West Virginia University but has discovered her passion for writing. Since her first published article in 2010, she now has over one hundred and fifty published articles and devotions.

Harriet is a member of American Christian Fiction Writers and Louisville Christian Writers. She and Shirley Crowder are co-authors of the holiday devotional *Glimpses of the Savior*, published by TMP Books in 2015.

Follow her on:

Website: www.harrietemichael.com

Facebook: https://www.facebook.com/harrietmichaelauthor

Blog: www.whatHehasdoneformysoul.blogspot.com

ALSO BY THE AUTHOR

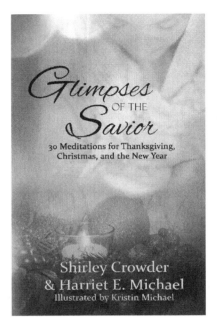

Finding Jesus among the Celebrations and Decorations

In early November, we get busy preparing for Thanksgiving, Christmas, and the New Year, and we often forget the real meanings behind these celebrations.

We can guard against this by preparing our hearts to seek Him as we focus on God's Word, and by remembering that Thanksgiving is a time to give God thanks; Christmas is the celebration of the Savior's birth; the New Year brings new beginnings. Then, as we go about doing the things the Lord has called us to do where He has called us to do them, we catch Glimpses of the Savior and biblical truth in the things we experience and observe.

These devotionals are based on memories of Thanksgiving, Christmas, and New Year celebrations in Africa and America. May the Holy Spirit work through these meditations to help readers recognize Glimpses of the Savior in the things they observe, and become skilled at finding Jesus among the celebrations and decorations.

Available on Kindle and in paperback from Amazon and most bookstores by request.

Made in the USA
Middletown, DE
09 July 2016